THE LIFE OF
COACH CHUCK CURTIS

THE LIFE OF
COACH CHUCK CURTIS

FROM THE SPREAD FORMATION

TO

SPREADING THE WORD

as told to Brian Honea

FOREWORD BY

ROGER WILLIAMS

TCU Press
Fort Worth, Texas

Library of Congress Cataloging-in-Publication Data

Curtis, Chuck, 1935- author.
 The life of coach Chuck Curtis : from the spread formation to spreading
the word / as told to Brian Honea
     pages cm
 ISBN 978-0-87565-603-8 (pbk. : alk. paper)
1. Curtis, Chuck, 1935- 2. Football coaches--Texas--Biography. 3. Quar-
terbacks (Football players)--Texas--Biography. I. Honea, Brian (Brian
James), 1971-II. Title.
 GV939.C88A3 2014
 796.332092--dc23
 [B]
                              2014011862

TCU Press
P.O. Box 298300
Fort Worth, Texas 76129
817.257.7822
www.prs.tcu.edu

To order books: 1.800.826.8911

Designed by Bill Brammer
www.fusion29.com

FOREWORD

As a young child growing up in Fort Worth, I remember watching the Horned Frogs play on Saturdays at Amon G. Carter Stadium. And there was Chuck leading the way as quarterback. He could do it all. He could run and he could pass. But mostly, he could lead. When Chuck stepped on the field, the Frogs knew where to look for leadership. And that leadership led all the way to the Cotton Bowl in 1956.

It wasn't until years later that I got to meet the man that I had respected for so long. I was playing baseball at TCU about ten years after Chuck had left and gone on to more greatness as a Texas high school football coach. He had always seemed bigger than life to me, watching him from the stands. Now, meeting him in person, I realized that he didn't just seem like a legend; he was one. He stood tall and strong; he spoke quietly and with a smile.

Over the years I got the chance to become friends with Chuck. And what I learned was that even though Chuck was a great player and a great coach, he was an even greater person. Will Rogers and Chuck Curtis would have gotten along well: neither one met a man he didn't like or a challenge he couldn't meet. When Chuck talked about overcoming obstacles in life, he made it clear that he didn't see them as stumbling blocks but rather as stepping stones.

And he was always winning—not just football games; he was winning people over, too. I remember the year he asked me to speak at the Lions Club Valentine's Dance in Mineral Wells. Who needs a speaker for a Valentine's party? I think it was Chuck's way of making a retired minor league baseball player like me feel included. That was Chuck—always building relationships and always adding to his team.

As a coach, Chuck's principle was that proper preparation would lead to a powerful performance. And he realized he wasn't just coaching his players about football; he was teaching them about life. Throughout his storied career as a Texas high school coach, he touched more lives and hearts than anyone I know. There are men living all across the country today that have successful lives because they learned how to game plan and take on adversity from playing for Coach Curtis.

One of the greatest moments of my own life was when I had the opportunity to inform Chuck that he had been inducted into the TCU Lettermen's Association Hall of Fame. The honor was well deserved and long overdue. Yet true to form, Chuck showed characteristic grace and humility. He looked down, paused, then said simply, "Thank you."

In the pages that follow, you will read about a great man who did great things on and off the field. You will be glad you read the book, just as I am glad to call him my friend.

Congressman Roger Williams
US Capitol
February 27, 2014

CHAPTER ONE

BEGINNINGS

Memories of the time I've spent with Coach Chuck Curtis over the past fifty years begin with the first time I saw him and heard him speak in the boys' gym at Garland High in the early spring of 1963.

When Chuck first came to Garland, I was a young sophomore who had pretty much given up on my plans to play football in high school in favor of baseball and basketball, until his words and his presence motivated me to abandon those two sports and take up football once more.

At the time it was probably a poor choice for me, because I hadn't had much success at the sport in the years previous. But I knew I wanted to play for Chuck because I was motivated by his positive attitude and self-confidence—two things I didn't have much of at that time.

Over the next two years, my teammates and I enjoyed incredible success—both collectively and individually. Most of my memories of those times aren't of the games, however, but of the practices and times spent listening to Chuck as he prepared us for each opponent. His presence in my life couldn't have come at a more opportune time for me because of the ways he encouraged us all and led us victoriously to achieve our common goal. Chuck taught me life lessons that I have used in all of the years that have since followed—lessons in self-discipline and sacrifice, and how to focus on the important aspects of the project at hand. I knew that he wasn't trying to inspire me individually, but he did that for me and my teammates by causing each one of us to know that jobs in the starting lineups were based on merit, and that we all had an equal chance to succeed based on our performances. For me, it was a revelation of truth, and it was all the inspiration I needed to do what I knew I must to become the player I wanted to be.

In the years that have followed our championships at Garland, my life has been blessed in so many ways it would be difficult to chronicle them all. It suffices to say that I played football in the Southwest Conference and the Big Eight as a scholarship athlete; played professional golf at the highest levels with some of the greatest players in the game; hosted my own syndicated radio and television series, and addressed thousands from the pulpit—but if the Lord were to give me the opportunity to relive any time in my life, I'd play football again for Chuck Curtis.

ROGER PARKER, *Associate Pastor, Second Baptist Church, Houston, Texas* *(Membership 56,000)*

The game of football is a lot like the game of life. Most of football is mental. If you've got a positive outlook and you're energized and having fun, you're not going to make stupid mistakes. If you're out there just to be out there, that shows up, and you won't be out there too long, playing for me. For my players at Jacksboro High School and at Garland High School, it just all came together. My players believed in what they were going to do. They believed they were going to win—and did they ever. My road to winning didn't start at Garland High School, or Jacksboro, or even at TCU where I played college football. It started in Midlothian, Texas, about thirty minutes southwest of Dallas, on July 15, 1935, during the Great Depression. Economic conditions were so bad that Ellis County, where Midlothian is located, had a 16 percent unemployment rate. My dad, John Curtis, was a farmer and a sharecropper. We had a little farm in Midlothian, but Daddy was able to get a better one outside of Cedar Hill just a few miles north of Midlothian, so we moved to Cedar Hill in the early '40s.

Our farm primarily produced cotton, but we also had corn and hay crops. When I was in the first grade and the roasting ears were ready, my job was to take our pair of mules and drive the wagon. I could really handle those mules. One of the main chores was to hoe around the cotton stalks so they would be clean and free of weeds. I was pretty young when I learned to sharpen a hoe. My job around the barn was basically taking care of the animals. I slopped the pigs and helped milk the cows. We always had one to three cows to milk. Dad would fill a bucket full of milk, and my job was to take it and get it on the back porch for Momma without spilling it. I had several other chores, like making

Bonnie Curtis, Chuck's mother, shown during the 1940s outside the Curtis home in Cedar Hill, Texas.

sure there was fresh water in the house. My dad showed a lot of faith in me even though I was only six or seven years old.

My sister had to take care of the chicken house in addition to her chores in the house. She took care of the eggs. We had chicken every Sunday, so we raised plenty of chickens.

We had so much cotton growing that my dad would go to the edge of Dallas where the African Americans who wanted to do day labor would gather. Eventually he had to buy a one-ton flatbed truck to carry everybody. And most of the time I'd ride shotgun with him. We'd go up there and get us a crew to pick the cotton and head back to the farm, and they'd work until just before dark.

There were usually a few African American kids tagging along that were my age, and we had lots of fun in the wagon. We'd help pack the cotton down so the wagon would hold more. I didn't know about segregation or anything like that even though this was the 1940s in the South. I was not brought up to think that way. I played with those boys a lot, and there wasn't anything

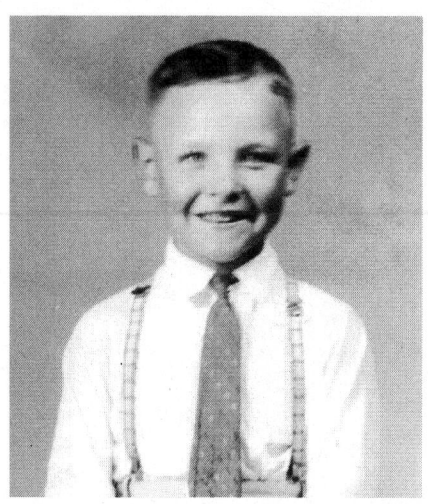

Charles Wayne "Chuck" Curtis,
about five years old, around 1940.

different or weird about it to me. We were a bad influence on each other, though. We worked hard, but it was fun. My mother Bonnie and my sister Edna Ruth, who was two years older than I was, would fix lunch and they would bring it out to us. We'd all take a break under the shade tree and have a big lunch. There was a plate for everybody, and that's just the way it was.

That year, around 1942, we had a big crop, and Daddy was able to buy our first tractor. One time, Dad had been using the tractor all day, and he drove it back under the shade of the tree. I don't know why, but for some reason he decided to drain the tractor's radiator. Apparently he thought that would help him speed up cooling down the tractor. He said to me as the scalding water gushed out of that radiator, "That water's hot. Stay away from it," and he went off to do something else. Well, he shouldn't have told me that, because I had to test it. I was barefoot—I didn't wear shoes until maybe the fourth grade, which was a couple of years after that. I stuck my toe under there and sure enough, those blisters started coming. I started running, and Daddy couldn't catch me to doctor it. Finally, I ran out of gas and he caught up with me. He stuck my foot under some coal oil—a common term for kerosene and an all-purpose home remedy in

The Curtis family with the members of the church in Cedar Hill, sometime in the early 1940s. John Curtis is at bottom left and Bonnie Curtis is at far right. Chuck is in the middle holding the banjo, and Chuck's sister, Edna Ruth, is sitting between Chuck and John, holding the mandolin.

those days. We doctored everything with coal oil back then. After I got some coal oil on it, I knew I was going to be okay.

I should have listened to my dad when he told me not to stick my foot in that hot water. But I didn't learn my lesson at that time. It was not until a few years later when I entered a local rodeo competition in Midlothian that I learned never to go against my dad's instructions.

This competition involved my uncle, my mother's brother, who lived about two miles from us. He was one of those "fun" guys. He talked me into chopping cotton and picking for him. He would pay me fifty cents a day, and Daddy wasn't paying me anything, so I took my uncle up on it.

At that time, Midlothian had an event called the Silver Dollar Rodeo, and one of the big events was a horse race. They called it the Silver Dollar Race because they paid out the prizes in silver dollars. My uncle had sold me on the fact that, if I wanted to ride a winner, then I needed to ride his horse instead of my dad's. So, I decided to ride my uncle's horse. When I got back home, I informed my dad of my decision. He told me that he had entered his horse in the race already, expecting me to ride it, and now he would have to find another jockey.

We lined up for the big race, and I got a head start on my uncle's horse. I was feeling pretty confident about my chances of winning. But once we got into the inside lane in the first curve, I could hear a horse breathing hard and coming up on us fast. I glanced around, and it was Daddy's horse. When we got to the back stretch, I was really whooping on my horse to get into high gear, but he had already given me all he had. Daddy's horse flew right by us. I felt pretty upset about that. When it was all over, I climbed off my uncle's horse, and I eased on over to Daddy and said, "I'll never go against you again, Dad. Never will."

My dad always knew best. He was a religious man, and he prayed a lot. He prayed so much trying to get a bumper crop (and everyone knew about it) that he prayed himself into being a preacher. His first preaching location was Sardis, a little town southeast of Midlothian, at an Assembly of God type of church. He not only preached at the church, he also played the guitar and sang. As a result of Daddy's preaching and service, that church group grew quickly. Daddy was quite a talented man, and I was proud that he was my dad.

He continued preaching at another church after we moved to Cedar Hill. Behind that little farm outside of Cedar Hill there was a creek. There was a place in the creek that had a hole that was deep enough to allow Daddy to baptize people. Daddy baptized me when I was in the first grade. That was an exciting day that I will always remember.

Daddy preached throughout all those years, and the congregations kept growing. A few years later, Daddy got the call to preach in Grand Prairie, which is between Dallas and Fort Worth, so right before I went into junior high, we moved. Mom and Daddy built the church in Grand Prairie where Daddy preached, and that membership grew quickly, too.

It was in Grand Prairie that my football career began. I started playing football while I was in the eighth grade. I had played all the sports that were available in the Cedar Hill elementary school, but football was not offered there.

My mother didn't want me to play football, because she was afraid I'd get hurt. Right as I was going into the seventh grade

The Curtis family on their front porch in Grand Prairie, circa 1947. Clockwise from top left: Bonnie Curtis, John Curtis, Edna Ruth Curtis, and Chuck (about twelve years old).

we made a deal that she'd get me a motor scooter if I didn't play football. I took her up on the deal. She got me the motor scooter and I didn't play football in seventh grade. The next year, however, I went out for the football team, because Mom and I didn't have a deal for the eighth grade. I got a motor scooter and I got to play football, so that turned into quite a deal for me. I didn't know how she would feel about me tricking her like that, but she eventually forgave me. She knew how I loved to play the game.

At first, I played end on the football team. The high school coach, Tom Pruitt, came to our practice one day to watch the eighth graders, because spring training was coming up. Coach Pruitt was going to move some of the eighth graders up to the high school level. He was there watching us to see who was good enough. I ran out for two or three passes and caught them. Each time I caught a pass, I threw the ball back to the player they'd chosen to be the quarterback. Coach Pruitt saw me throw the ball, and he called out, "Just a minute over there, Slim. Let me back up, and you throw me the ball." He backed up, and I fired him a perfect spiral. When he saw that, he declared, "I don't need you to catch any more. From this point on, you're going to be a quarterback." And I was—through high school, college, and the pros. My

Chuck with his mother, Bonnie, in Gainesville in the early 1950s, when Chuck was in high school.

position switch led to a name change. Up until the eighth grade, everyone called me Charles or Charles Wayne. When I became a quarterback, my sister, Edna Ruth, nicknamed me "Chuck." She thought that Chuck sounded more like a quarterback's name than Charles Wayne. Thanks to Edna Ruth, I've been known as Chuck ever since.

In the summer of 1950, just before my sophomore year of high school, we moved from Grand Prairie to Gainesville, up in North Texas. I'd discovered I had a real talent for playing quarterback, and I was lucky enough to continue to do that at Gainesville High School.

About this time, I got a job working on an oil rig, and with the money I earned, I bought a 1950 Ford. It was a turquoise and black two-door hardtop. I had it all decked out. My dad was now the pastor at the Assembly of God Church in Gainesville, and that car was a good way to get my friends to go to church. I would go pick up my buddies from the football team and haul them to church in that Ford.

Every Sunday, the whole back row in church was made up of Gainesville High School footballers. When Daddy would start to preach, he'd close his eyes. Since we sat right next to the back door, about half of us usually tried to slip out. My dad put a stop to that when he faked us out one Sunday probably in late '51 or early '52, my junior year. He lowered his head, but he didn't close his eyes. He kept his eyes on us. When he saw us start to slip out, he said, "Charles Wayne, you and ol' Rusty sit down. You're going to get to hear today's sermon." We sat down, and he continued on with his sermon. That really embarrassed us.

As a result of that incident, my dad made me sing a solo in church soon after. Since my dad was the pastor, my family was responsible for the music at each service. Daddy played acoustic guitar and sang. He and my mother sang duets together. My sister Edna Ruth sang solos and played several instruments. She started out playing piano accordion, then went to accordion, then to the piano, and then to steel guitar. Whatever we needed, she could play and play very well. Everybody in my family except me was contributing to the church's music in some way. So Daddy gave

Chuck and his older sister, Edna Ruth, shown here in Gainesville in the early 1950s, once combined for a rousing rendition of "He's My Rock, My Sword, My Shield" in church.

me the biblical Word—he told me to get my butt in gear and to carry my weight.

The week leading up to my first Sunday solo passed by too quickly. When I got up to the front of the congregation to sing my song, my sister played an introduction on the piano, and I couldn't get anything out. She tried it again, and I still couldn't sing anything. I looked out into the congregation, and those eyeballs were all fixed on me. Daddy came up and put his arm around me and said, "I'll tell you what, folks. He will sing next Sunday. I want you to invite your neighbors, friends, cousins, aunts and uncles, and all your kinfolk, because he is going to sing."

The next week was the fastest week ever. This time Edna Ruth helped coach me. She said, "Look over their heads, and they won't know you're not looking right at them. Sing just like you were singing in the shower."

With Edna Ruth's help, I got through it. I sang a traditional gospel song, "He's My Rock, My Sword, My Shield," which was popularized many years later by country singer Randy Travis. I

Years after performing together in church in Gainesville, Chuck and his sister, Edna Ruth, joined together for another tune in the early 1980s.

was so proud of myself—I really felt like I'd pulled it off. After I sang, I went to the back row to sit with my buddies, and my best friend Homer Fuller, who lived around the corner from me, leaned over and said, "I thought you sounded better last Sunday."

I wasn't musically talented like my sister was; I had to work at it. I tried several instruments. I started out in junior high in Grand Prairie playing a coronet or trumpet because they didn't have any stringed instruments. But I didn't take to the brass instruments too well, so I quit.

Things were different in Gainesville. Most all the instruments at the church were stringed instruments. Daddy had me try out a mandolin and a banjo. I took lessons, and once I got the basics down I could halfway play. Daddy came across an upright bass in a pawnshop, and he brought it home for me. I started playing with it and discovered I had another talent that I would cultivate for the rest of my life. The upright bass was the one instrument I really took to. It seemed lots easier for me to be in rhythm when I played the upright bass. I didn't know it at the time, but I had an excellent ear for music. So I went into the bass-playing business. Now I could finally do what Daddy had wanted me to do when he gave me the Word and told me I needed to pull my own weight.

Getting that upright bass is what got me going in music. I did most all of my playing at church at first. When I got to college at TCU, I formed a band with some of my classmates, and we started playing at fraternities and at banquets and events like that. We mostly played western swing music.

That upright bass was made in Germany. I've had it insured, and it's worth between four and five thousand dollars now. Daddy probably paid less than a hundred dollars for it back in the '50s.

I continued to play football throughout high school. I wanted to finish out high school in Gainesville, even though my folks moved to Taylor, which is close to Austin in Central Texas, when I was a senior. They moved so my dad could preach at a bigger church.

I stayed in Gainesville, lived in a garage apartment, and paid my own way. I drove that 1950 Ford, and I shined it around Gainesville and Cooke County. My friends and I had a little fun with the folks gone. We'd fill up the front and back seat and head for the Red River for some of that Oklahoma three-two beer, instead of the strong six-point stuff. You could buy it legally in Oklahoma when you were eighteen. One quart of that would take care of the fully-loaded-down Ford.

In order to pay my bills, I was roughnecking with the morning tour on an oil rig in Cooke County, just west of Gainesville. Since I was underage, my dad had to sign a form that declared me to be an adult. He had to "give me away," so to speak. Roughnecking put me in a dangerous working environment, but it really built up some arm strength. We would use a piece of pipe attached to the drill bit to drill the hole. Hopefully we would reach some oil, and if we did, we would check with a specialist on site to see if we had enough oil. If we did not, we had to add more pipe and keep drilling deeper. That's called tripping a well. Once we had drilled deep enough, we had to pull all that pipe out of the hole and stack it standing up off to the side. We'd go down into the hole, however far it was, take all that pipe out, and stack it. There was a guy working above in the derrick and two or three on the floor to help move the pipe out of the hole because it was so heavy. You always had to have enough pipe stacked up standing for the man who was working up in the derrick, so we could add it quickly if we needed to drill deeper. I made $1.40 an hour, and that was good money in those days.

But I was still in high school, and football was my main focus. We played Paris High School in a district game that year. Paris had a player named Gene Stallings. When he went on to play in college at Texas A&M, Stallings was one of Bear Bryant's "Junction Boys," and later he became the head coach for A&M, an assistant coach for the Dallas Cowboys under Tom Landry, and the head coach of the St. Louis Cardinals of the NFL. After leaving the Cardinals, Stallings returned to college football and became the head coach at Alabama. Just like his college coach, Bear Bryant, Stallings was known for his toughness. It was fun playing against Stallings in high school, but he was tough then, too.

One of our big rivals was Greenville, a town to the southeast of Gainesville. In 1952 we faced them late in the regular season on Thanksgiving Day. In the last minute of the game we had the ball on about the fifty-yard line, and I threw it as far as I could. Roddy Osborne, our receiver who was also a backup quarterback, caught it for a touchdown, and we beat them. That was an exciting day for all of us.

We ended up winning the district championship and made the state playoffs in Class 3A. I was then selected to play in the Greenbelt Bowl in Childress, Texas, in the summer of '53. The Greenbelt Bowl was a high school all-star football game between the East and West all-stars in Texas. The Texas Christian University coach, the legendary Abe Martin, was the coach of the East all-stars, which was my team. The coach for the West team was none other than Sammy Baugh, a former TCU all-American, who had just returned to Texas after a legendary career with the Washington Redskins. My senior year in high school, I wore

In Gainesville, circa 1953, Chuck's senior year of high school.

Sammy Baugh's number thirty-three.

As it turned out, everyone on my team fell in love with Coach Martin and his philosophy. He made the game seem like it wasn't just a lot of hard work—it was fun, too. It was especially fun that day, when our team beat Sammy Baugh's all-stars, 7-6.

Six or seven of the high school all-stars there were sold on the Horned Frogs. TCU was in Fort Worth, only about an hour and a half drive from Gainesville. When the Greenbelt Bowl was over, we told Coach Martin that TCU was where we wanted to go to college.

Coach Martin called me a day or two after the game and asked if he could come up and visit with me. He drove up to Gainesville and sat right down beside me on the porch swing in front of our house, and he started talking about TCU. He had me look him right in the eye and tell him what I wanted to do, and I

Chuck with his dad, John Curtis, and his brother-in-law,
Morgan Thompson, in Colorado in the mid-1950s.

told him, "I want to go to TCU." He said, "That's great."

We visited for a while after that, and then he took off. At the
end of the day, I was excited and exhausted. I had to get to bed
early and head out to the oil rig at the crack of dawn the next
morning.

The guy who owned that rig happened to be a big University
of Oklahoma supporter. After the all-star game, he started trying to change my mind to get me to go to Oklahoma University
and play for Bud Wilkinson. OU had a fifty-seven-game winning
streak going at that time. My boss said I could work on that rig
as long as I wanted to if I would just commit to Oklahoma.

I called Coach Martin and told him I got a chance for a better summer job working for the OU folks. He said, "Go ahead and take the job. I know where you're going to school." He still had every confidence that I would play for him at TCU. A few days passed by, and the OU guy kept me pumped up. So I called Coach Martin again and told him, "I changed my mind and I want to go to OU." He still was unfazed. He simply asked me, "Where are you at right now?" I answered, "I'm on the porch swing." He quickly replied, "Don't get off it. I'm driving your way and I'll be there as soon as I can get there."

Coach Martin made the hour and a half drive to Gainesville from Fort Worth, pulled up, parked, and got out. I was already sitting on the swing, and he sat down beside me. He asked me, "Chuck-a-luck, last time we were here, and we were sitting on this swing, what did you tell me?" I responded, "I told you I was going to TCU." He said, slapping me on the knee, "That's good enough for me." He got up, got in his car, and drove off. I was still sitting there thinking about that pat on the knee. By the time he got back to Fort Worth, I called him and said, "Coach, you got me. I'm going to TCU." I just had to stick to my word.

CHAPTER TWO

PLAYING DAYS

When you play against runners as good as (Jim) Swink and (Buddy) Dike, it's awfully hard to stop a fine passer like Curtis. . . . Curtis is just about the best passer I have seen this fall.

JIM BROWN, *Football Hall of Famer and former Syracuse star, speaking to the press after the 1957 Cotton Bowl between Syracuse and TCU.*

W e had a fine freshman team at TCU when I first got there. Back then, the freshmen had to play on the freshman team. You couldn't play on varsity until your sophomore year. TCU had all those all-stars from the Greenbelt Bowl on the freshman team, so I liked our chances of winning.

We were not just top-notch football players, we were also top-notch athletes. Some of us formed an outlaw fast-pitch softball team. Softball was pretty big back then. I mainly pitched on the team, but I also played first base, catcher, and shortstop; I was a utility man. We called the team Abe's Aces, after Coach Martin, and we'd play whoever we could get to play us and play wherever we could. We weren't in any league; we just played outlaw. Some of the good pitchers made a lot of money. It was unorganized, but each town pretty much had a softball league or at least a team back then.

All of us were pretty talented athletes in just about every sport we tried, but that's probably because we worked hard at it. We were good enough that during basketball season we started up a team that won the state championship in the Texas Amateur Athletic Federation. We loved every sport we played.

The TAAF championship basketball team gathered for a reunion some fifty years after winning the title. Chuck is pictured third from right.

TCU's freshman football team, known as the Wogs, nearly beat TCU's varsity Horned Frogs in a scrimmage in the fall of 1953 with Chuck at quarterback. He wore number 11 as a freshman, and is pictured on the back row near the middle. *Courtesy Special Collections, Mary Couts Burnett Library, TCU.*

The 1953-54 Wogs were not just great football players, they were great athletes. The Wog track team in the spring of 1954 included several members of the football team. Chuck is the tallest one on the back row. *Courtesy Special Collections, Mary Couts Burnett Library, TCU.*

The first time TCU's freshman football team scrimmaged against the varsity, we moved right on down the field and scored. The coach stopped it then and there, because he didn't want those upperclassmen whoopin' on us little ol' freshmen later.

I loved playing for Abe Martin. When I played quarterback for TCU in the 1950s, Abe Martin was the most popular man in Fort Worth. He was an extremely wise man. He always had a wide grin. He was a cool customer who'd chew on an old cigar and sit with his feet propped up. He didn't get too excited about anything. He was the same if we were winning by a hundred or losing by a hundred, not that we ever lost by a hundred. And he never cussed; he used the word "schistopot," and that was the closest he ever came. We declared that to be cussing even though it wasn't, because we didn't want him to be perfect.

As a freshman at TCU, late 1953/early 1954.

After starting at quarterback my freshman year, I moved up to the varsity team and became the starter there as a sophomore. I was the starting quarterback for the remainder of my tenure at TCU, and only once did I ever go against Coach Martin's instructions. We were playing Baylor in Waco in 1955, my junior year. Our defense stopped Baylor on about the two-yard line, and our offense took over.

I called all the plays as the quarterback, but on this occasion Abe Martin sent the punter, Ray Taylor, into the huddle with a play, and one of our halfbacks went out. It was third down and twelve. Taylor informed me that Coach Martin wanted us to punt, but since he didn't give instructions as to when we were supposed to punt, I determined that first I was going to run at least a couple of my plays to give the punter some breathing room.

On the first play, we popped it out of there. Then before Abe could get too excited, I called another play from the line of scrimmage and we got a first down, and we went down to the other end of the field and scored a touchdown.

We went on to win the game, 28-6.

As the game ended and I was coming off the field, I saw Abe coming toward me through the crowd, and he looked like he

Chuck, second from left, with his ROTC group at TCU in the mid-1950s. *Courtesy Special Collections, Mary Couts Burnett Library, TCU.*

wanted to tell me something. He stuck his arm around me and said, "Right now, your mom and dad think I'm congratulating you on this game. But if you hadn't made that first down and made a touchdown, I would have kicked your ass!" And he didn't cuss.

I got along with Abe Martin really well. I got along with all my coaches because I wanted to be a coach. I was heavily involved in watching, learning, and seeing how they put it all together. I was fortunate to have some great teachers when I played football.

When I was a sophomore in 1954, we played Penn State and beat them, 20-7. At the time Penn State had a couple of really fine players. One was Lenny Moore, who was a receiver and a break-away-type runner, and later he was an all-pro for the Baltimore Colts for several years. The other was their big lineman, Rosey Grier, who was later my teammate with the New York Giants. We were fortunate that we stopped Moore from scoring and we hung on to win. It turned out that these two players made a little history that day, although we didn't know it at the time. Lenny Moore and Rosey Grier were the first two African Americans ever to play in Amon G. Carter Stadium, where TCU played its home games.

Chuck, shown here as a freshman with TCU in the fall of 1953, had been a quarterback since the eighth grade. *Courtesy Special Collections, Mary Couts Burnett Library, TCU.*

As a sophomore in the fall of 1954, Curtis became the starting quarterback for the varsity Horned Frogs. He is shown here on the third row just left of center wearing number 46, which was the number he wore for the remainder of his TCU career. *Courtesy Special Collections, Mary Couts Burnett Library, TCU.*

The Southwest Conference was at the top of the mountain at that time, and every game was a tough game. One of our toughest opponents within the conference was Texas A&M. Bear Bryant was the head coach, and he was the "King Bee" among college coaches. Bryant had a great team, and he did a wonderful job there. My junior year they beat us, 19-16, and it was our only loss in the regular season.

Chuck as a junior at TCU, 1955-56.
Courtesy Special Collections,
Mary Couts Burnett Library, TCU.

One of our non-conference games my junior year was against Alabama, whose quarterback was Bart Starr. Our defense, which included many of the same players as our offense, was feeling at the top of their game. The weather was nice, and it was a great day to play football. We were ready to play them. We received the opening kickoff and completed several passes, and we rolled right on down and scored. That gave us a lift. We ended up shutting out the Crimson Tide, 21-0. Starr went on to have a hall of fame career with Green Bay under Vince Lombardi, but he didn't really jump out at me as a great player when he was in college. I'm guessing he was maturing right about then.

In spite of our loss to A&M, TCU won the Southwest Conference that year, for the first time in four years. At the end of the season, on January 2, 1956, we played Ole Miss in the Cotton Bowl. We had an all-American running back named Jim Swink. Before the opening kickoff, Coach Martin told me, "They'll probably kick it to you, because you're the slowest thing back there.

Chuck, number 46 at far right, has just handed the ball off to Buddy Dike, who is running behind the blocking of Norman Hamilton, number 75.
Courtesy Special Collections, Mary Couts Burnett Library, TCU.

When you get it, you pitch it to Swink and let him run it back." That was fine with me, because I didn't want to run it back.

Sure enough, they kicked off to me. But they kicked short, and I caught it just barely before it hit the ground. I was 6-foot-5, 205 pounds. I was going so fast, I was out of control, and all of a sudden I got hit from every angle. That put me out of the game. Injured shoulder, broken ribs, hurt pride, and all. . . . That was really the first time I'd ever been hurt playing football. We lost the game by one point, 14-13.

That play against Ole Miss in the Cotton Bowl and one play against Texas A&M my senior year are two plays that haunt me to this day.

When we played Texas A&M my senior year, I looked at that game as a chance to get back at the Aggies for giving us our only loss of the regular season the year before. And we were going to get a chance to do it on their home field at College Station, which is about a three-hour drive south of Fort Worth.

We squared off against A&M on October 20, 1956, in the fourth game of the season for what became known in TCU lore

Playing quarterback for TCU, Chuck gets ready to throw a block for
TCU all-American Jim Swink (left, with ball) during the now-famous
"Hurricane Game" between TCU and Texas A&M at College Station,
October 20, 1956. Notice the storm brewing in the sky overhead.
Photo by Al Panzera, courtesy Fort Worth Star-Telegram *Photograph Collection,
Special Collections, University of Texas at Arlington Library, Arlington, Texas.*

as the "Hurricane Game." It was billed as a battle between two
undefeated teams that featured superstar running backs—Jim
Swink for TCU and John David Crow for A&M. A&M's quarterback, Roddy Osborne, happened to be a former high school
teammate of mine at Gainesville.

The sun was shining when the game started. From there it
went to raining and then to hailing, hence the "Hurricane Game."
Play was even halted in the second quarter for a while. Late in
the game, we were driving down the field well, even while the
hail and rain pelted us, and we got down to a first and goal from
about the six-yard line. Our best shot to score was handing off to
Jim Swink, so he ran in there three times using the same play—
but he gained a total of only five yards on those three plays. Now
it was fourth down and goal from the one.

I called the same play again in the huddle, which was a handoff to Swink, and he runs right. As I was coming up to the line of
scrimmage after we broke out of the huddle, I saw A&M over-

loading the line of scrimmage. They were anticipating another handoff to Swink, so I decided to change the play. I yelled to my line and backs that I was going to bootleg it, but none of them could hear me because it was raining so hard and hailing on our helmets. As loud as I could, I hollered to Swink and whoever could hear, "I'm changing the play to the bootleg." But Swink couldn't hear me because of the noise. In fact, nobody heard me.

Because nobody heard me, I couldn't run the bootleg. So I ran the play we called in the huddle. Swink actually made it into the end zone but he didn't get credit for it. At that time, you had to do more than just break the plane of the goal line to score a touchdown. You had to have from your waist on up in the end zone before the officials would count it. Also, A&M's coach, Bear Bryant, was tough on the officials, and I think they gave him a lot of slack.

What made it worse is that I could have just walked into the end zone if I'd called the bootleg. Everything ended up on the right side, because the A&M players knew Swink was going to run that way, and I planned to bootleg it to the left. I looked over to the left and there was nobody there. It's more than fifty years later, and I haven't gotten that play cleared out of my mind yet.

Not scoring that touchdown proved to be the difference, because Texas A&M won, 7-6. But even though A&M won the battle, TCU still won the war. A&M ended that season with a 9-0-1 record, and they won the Southwest Conference, but they were disqualified from playing in the Cotton Bowl because of recruiting violations. As a result of A&M's ineligibility, TCU received the Cotton Bowl bid even though we finished the regular season 7-3 and didn't win the Southwest Conference.

In spite of what happened in that A&M game, I played some great games my senior year. I went into that season determined to make up for getting knocked out of the Cotton Bowl against Ole Miss on the opening kickoff. Two of the best games I had as a senior were in the 1957 Cotton Bowl against Syracuse and in conference play against the Texas Longhorns.

Against the University of Texas my senior year, I threw four long touchdown passes, each to different receivers. At the time,

Against Baylor on November 3, Chuck (46) got to carry the ball with Bobby Jack Oliver of Baylor (76) in pursuit. Converging on the play are Vernon Uecker (74) of TCU and Paul Dickson (71) of Baylor. TCU won the game, 7-6. *Photo by John Lee, courtesy* Fort Worth Star-Telegram *Photograph Collection, Special Collections, University of Texas at Arlington Library, Arlington, Texas.*

Texas had a brand new young head coach from Oklahoma named Darrell Royal. He went on to achieve legendary status, winning three national championships as the Longhorns' head coach. But on November 17, 1956, we had his number. We beat them, 46-0, on our home field. His Longhorn teams lost only forty-seven games in the twenty years he coached there, and that loss had to be one of the most lopsided for him. That win was especially meaningful for us because we were 4-3 heading into that game, coming off a tough loss to Texas Tech. We desperately needed to beat the Longhorns to stay in the hunt.

After beating Texas, we won our final two regular season games against Rice and Southern Methodist, and we earned the Cotton Bowl bid after Texas A&M was declared ineligible. The 1957 Cotton Bowl against Syracuse was TCU's ninth bowl game, which at the time was the most of any team in the Southwest Conference. In that game, I threw for two touchdowns and

The 1956 TCU Horned Frogs made it back to the Cotton Bowl with Chuck in his third year at quarterback. This time, the Horned Frogs were victorious over Jim Brown and Syracuse. Curtis is number 46 on the back row, slightly left of center. *Courtesy Special Collections, Mary Couts Burnett Library, TCU.*

ran for one more. I made several tackles on football legend Jim Brown while playing safety on defense. We tried to hit him as many times as we could. If we slowed him down a little bit, the rest of the defense came in to try to get a lick on him. We really did an excellent job of it. He covered a lot of ground, but we contained him and it took him a long time to get down the field and score.

There was no shadow of a doubt that Jim Brown was going to be a star in the NFL. He did it all for Syracuse in the Cotton Bowl that day. He ran the ball, kicked off, punted, and kicked the extra points. He scored three of their four touchdowns. Thank goodness we got to block one of his extra points, because that was the difference in a 28-27 game.

Chico Mendoza was the one who blocked the point for us. He was from Ranger High School in Ranger, which is in Central Texas, about eighty miles from Fort Worth. He was average sized, about 190 pounds, but he was a solid player. His team at Ranger had won the 2A state championship a few years earlier, and Chico was named all-state. Chico was probably the best-

TCU head football coach Abe Martin, far right, discusses strategy with his quarterbacks in practice on December 31, 1956, the day before the Horned Frogs beat Jim Brown's Syracuse team at the Cotton Bowl. From left, Hunter Enis, Dick Finney, and Chuck. *Photo by Al Panzera, courtesy* Fort Worth Star-Telegram *Photograph Collection, University of Texas at Arlington Library, Arlington, Texas.*

looking young man on our team. Girls loved him. He was funny, he was good-looking, and he was a great conversationalist.

One of our defensive linemen, Norman Hamilton, had a great game for us that day. We called him "The Animal." He got through and tackled the Syracuse quarterback several times. The Syracuse team kept trying to double team Hamilton, and I think that's how Chico got through to block the extra point. I was on my wingside blocking on that play. Chico wasn't named most valuable player of the game, but to us he did the most valuable thing.

Jim Brown was chosen most valuable player of the game, and that ticked me off because I had the best game of my career—and not only that, I felt like the MVP should have come from the

TCU's twenty senior football players gathered in practice the week before the Cotton Bowl game against Syracuse. From left, the ten players on the top of the pyramid are Vernon Halbeck, cocaptain; Don Cooper; Vernon Uecker; Frank Windegger; Jim Swink, cocaptain; Kenneth Wineburg; Paul Harvard; Harold Pollard; Joe Williams, captain; Bill (Skippy) Few. Center pyramid: Orville Neal; Henry Crowsey; Neil Hoskins; O'Day Williams; Chuck Curtis; Jack Webb; Jay Ray McCullough. Base: John Nikkle; Norman Hamilton, and Don Sanford. *Photo by Al Panzera, courtesy* Fort Worth Star-Telegram *Photograph Collection, University of Texas at Arlington Library, Arlington, Texas.*

winning team. I threw two touchdown passes and ran for one more. I completed twelve out of fifteen passes for one hundred and seventy-four yards. I told the press after the game, "Those receivers were getting open, and there was mighty good protection. With that, a passer doesn't have to do much." I wanted my teammates to get all the credit they deserved.

The game was not as close as it sounded, even though it was 28-27. We jumped out in front and were in control really all the way through the game. We were geared up a little bit more after Chico blocked the extra point. We didn't let them get close enough to try a field goal. Jim Brown was kicking extra points, so I guess he would have been the one to try for the field goal if they had gotten close enough, but they never got close enough. That was an exciting game for the fans and for all those involved.

We were probably more prepared mentally and physically for that game than any of the other games we played at TCU in the four years I was there. Everything was working for us that day.

We were sharp mentally, we were quick, and we didn't make any glaring mistakes.

My center, Joe Williams, and I had been selected to play in the Senior Bowl in Mobile, Alabama. Joe played high school football for Greenville, Texas, which was a big rival of my high school, Gainesville. As soon as that Cotton Bowl game against Syracuse was over, Joe and I caught a plane for Mobile, but we were late getting in at New Orleans, and we had to spend the night there. We didn't know it until we got off the plane, but our ride to the hotel from the airport was Paul Brown. At that time, he was the coach and the owner of the Cleveland Browns. He picked us up in his limo, and we got to go over the plays while we were in the car. I started that game for the South all-stars against the North in the Senior Bowl, and I threw the winning touchdown pass. Joe Williams played center for me—Coach Brown wanted a center that was from the same team as the quarterback so that there wouldn't be any fumbles in an all-star game. The communication between Joe and me was so clear that we never had any problems on the exchange.

My junior year I had been named All-Southwest Conference. At the end of my senior season, I won the Dan D. Rogers MVP Award, which is the award given out annually to the most valuable player on TCU's football team. The winner is picked by the coaches. I was tickled to death to win that award because we had some great players who had great years. Among them was our all-American, Jim Swink. We also had O'Day Williams, who was a receiver with speed and great hands. He is also a buddy of mine who coached with me later at Garland High School.

TCU's combined record my junior and senior years was 17-5 with two straight Cotton Bowl appearances, including one victory. When we lost, we didn't lose by much. Two of those five losses were by one point, and another was by three points. In 1993, I was inducted into the TCU Lettermen's Association Hall of Fame. I worked hard at being the best, so when it turned out that I made the hall of fame, I felt I earned it.

My play at TCU caught the attention of some professional teams. In the spring of 1957, both the New York Giants of the

National Football League and the Winnipeg Blue Bombers of the Canadian Football League drafted me. I signed with Winnipeg because they offered me more money. I got a $2,500 bonus and a $12,500 contract. That summer, I took that $2,500 bonus and went to the Ford dealership and bought a brand new 1957 Ford Fairlane 500, and paid $2,500 cash for it. It was a coral sand and white two-door hardtop with air conditioning underneath the dash. I just got in it and headed north, and I went as far as I could until I ran right into Winnipeg.

At the time, Bud Grant was in his first year as head coach at Winnipeg. Later he coached the Minnesota Vikings and became the only coach to be elected to both the Pro Football Hall of Fame in Canton and the Canadian Football Hall of Fame. We had quite a team in Winnipeg in 1957. I had to compete with two or three other quarterbacks for the starting job. One of them was Kenny Ploen, and he was from Iowa. It took about three or four weeks before Coach Grant moved me up to starting quarterback. Toward the end of the season, sometimes Grant would shuttle quarterbacks in and out on every other play. I'd run a play, then I'd go out, and Kenny Ploen would come in and run a play and come out, and then I'd go back in.

I liked Bud Grant. He was a players' coach. He would always stand behind his players. He was an outdoorsman, and we talked a lot about hunting and fishing. He never cracked under pressure and he never lost his temper. He was in total control of himself. He was low-key, but he wanted all of your ability. That was all he wanted. If you didn't hustle or if you weren't giving one hundred percent, he would let you know it quickly.

Toward the end of the 1957 season, Winnipeg was getting ready to play in the Grey Cup, the Canadian Football League's championship game, and two of our running backs were hurt. Coach Grant didn't think we had much of a chance without them. So he sent one of his assistants to get me, and he told me to go see Coach Grant and bring my playbook. That concerned me, because when the coach wants you to see him and bring your playbook, that's like bringing your keys and turning them in. I thought it was going to be bad news for sure. When I got there,

Grant said, "This is probably going to be the first trade between the NFL and the Canadian league." They were trading me to the New York Giants for two running backs so they could have a chance in the Grey Cup. They lost the Grey Cup that year to Hamilton, but they won it in four of the next five years under Grant.

I didn't know it at the time, but that trade was the greatest thing that ever happened to me because of the coaching I received and what I learned about being a coach that helped me later on.

When I joined the Giants in September 1957, I had no idea who their coaches were. Jim Lee Howell, from Arkansas, was the head coach. He was a smooth talker, and he made me feel comfortable. He started introducing me to the assistant coaches. He said, "Tom Landry is our defensive coach, and Vince Lombardi is our offensive coach, and you'll be working with them."

At the time, I had no idea about the caliber of coaches we had with the Giants. This was 1957, and both Landry and Lombardi were still a few years away from achieving football immortality as head coaches with the Cowboys and Packers, respectively. I didn't know much about them before I joined the Giants, but I soon found out there were none better than those two. And I was going to be able to sit at the table and learn from them.

I was the backup quarterback to Charlie Conerly. When I first saw Charlie, I thought he was a coach. He was smoking in the dressing room, and that was unheard of. He had some age on him—he looked like he was fifty to me—but I guess he was in his late thirties. He could still play. He couldn't move around too well, but he still had a strong arm.

I didn't get to play much that year, but I had a neat job as long as Conerly stayed in there and stayed healthy. The coach who was the lowest on the totem pole had to go to the top of Yankee Stadium, where we played our home games, with an instant Polaroid camera and take the shots of the opponent's defense and offense. Then he put the pictures in a sock with a rock, tied a knot in it, and threw it down to the field. My job was to catch that sock with the rock in it so that none of the first-string players got hurt. Then I had to go over and diagram what was in the picture on the blackboard for Coach Lombardi. This was high tech back then.

The fans were crazy up in New York. They loved watching me catch those socks on the sideline. I made spectacular catches, and I even had my own cheering section. The younger group behind the bench closest to us would always holler and cheer when I'd make one of those catches.

One day in practice just before we went to work out, Lombardi called a team meeting and said, "I want you all to listen up. Ol' Tex over here has been doing those spectacular catches down there, and he's got the crowd all riled up, and it's making us lose our focus. I have a presentation to make. Come up here, Tex. I've got an award here. As far as I know, this is the only award the New York Giants have ever given in this type of situation. I'm going to present to him a butterfly net so that he won't be making those spectacular catches. He can just stick it out there and it'll fall in there, and he can get back over there to the blackboard without the crowd upsetting our players and us losing our focus."

I don't know of any other New York Giant who has ever been issued a butterfly net.

The Giants had a really strong team in 1957. In fact, they had won the NFL championship in 1956 by routing the Chicago Bears. We had players like Frank Gifford, Sam Huff, Rosey Brown, Rosey Grier, Kyle Rote, Andy Robustelli, and Dick Nolan. Gifford, Huff, and Brown are all in the hall of fame now.

I was thankful for players like Frank Gifford and Sam Huff. Gifford became well known as a broadcaster on *Monday Night Football* for so many years. He stood up for me once by telling Lombardi, "Coach, don't cut Tex. If you do, I'll have the skinniest legs of anybody on the team. Right now, he has that honor, and we want him to keep that honor."

Frank Gifford and Sam Huff coached me a little bit the first day I was in practice. While I was getting suited up, they told me, "Lombardi will be chewing on your butt whether you think you deserve it or not, and you've got to let it go in one ear and out the other. You just take it and go on." That's the way it happened. If

I missed a pass, or if Conerly threw a bad pass, Lombardi would chew me out because Conerly didn't do it right. He didn't want to chew Conerly out in front of the team and me.

Lombardi really liked to chew on people. You could be a half a block away from him and you could still hear him. It wasn't harmful, he just liked to do it, and it was successful for him, too. When Lombardi stepped up to say something, we all got to shiverin' and a shakin', but we were ready to do whatever he wanted us do. We would have run through a burning building if he'd asked us to.

Lombardi was the kind of coach that would make you a better player. One example of that is Bart Starr, who wasn't so impressive as a college player. But Starr had an outstanding career under Lombardi at Green Bay. The Packers won the first two Super Bowls, and Starr was named most valuable player of both games.

Eventually, Lombardi lightened up on me and stopped chewing me out. I don't know why. Maybe he was testing me early to see if I could handle him and see if I had any pride or backtalk in me. I respected him, and I just accepted the chew outs and continued playing. I wanted to stay, and I wanted to play.

In fact, I found out that Lombardi even had a soft side to him. He had a heart after all. He gave me a chance to leave the team in the middle of the season to see the birth of my daughter.

When I was drafted by Winnipeg, my first wife, Sue, went up there with me, and she had just become pregnant. Her folks came up for a vacation to see where we were. We decided we'd rather have a Texan than a Canadian, so my in-laws took Sue back to Gainesville. Shortly after that, Winnipeg traded me to the Giants for those running backs. So when I took off for New York, they were back in Gainesville.

The Giants were just finishing up their preseason in upstate New York when I got there. They probably had a week or so left. During that time, I mentioned to one of the players that my wife just had a big gal, my daughter Kimberly. I told him, "Man, I've got a brand new daughter just born." And he said, "Well, shoot, we've got to celebrate."

It wasn't long before the news reached Lombardi. He came to me one day in practice when we were in Detroit getting ready to play a preseason game against the Lions, and he said, "Tex, come here. Don't tell nobody, but here's you a round-trip ticket from Detroit to Dallas-Fort Worth to go check on that big baby gal that you've got. I'll tell you what we'll do. We'll grab your uniform, and you'll fly back to meet us in Detroit." He was really concerned, and I found out that he was about families and togetherness and those types of things. So I got to see both sides of Lombardi.

I stayed two or three days in Gainesville, then I got back to Detroit in time for the Sunday game. Bobby Layne, from Highland Park near Dallas, was the quarterback for Detroit. Charlie Conerly got knocked woozy, and I guess Coach Lombardi just wanted to show me off. He called me over and said, "Tex, you still remember that offense we used to run?"

I answered, "Yes, sir."

"Well, get in there."

So I went in and played about half the game. We won, and Conerly didn't have to go back in.

My relationship with baseball legend Mickey Mantle started when I was with the Giants and he was with the Yankees around that time in 1957; both the Giants and the Yankees played their home games in Yankee Stadium and mine and Mickey's lockers were close to each other.

On days when we were working out in shorts and going over plays, I'd slip him onto the field and he'd catch passes from me. In fact, I think he could have started for the Giants as a wide receiver. He had soft hands, quickness, and strength in his arms.

Casey Stengel, the manager of the Yankees, caught us throwing the football around one day and said to me, "Tex, I'll tell you one thing. If you get Mantle hurt, I'll knock you all the way back to Texas." I told Casey, "Ok, if it's a tight jam, I'll overthrow him."

During the Giants' practices, I learned a great deal by watching players react to the difference in personalities between Vince

Lombardi and Tom Landry. There was a kid on the team who had gotten down and out, and Lombardi was chewing on him all the time. Just as soon as Lombardi eased away from that kid and got out of the way, Landry came in behind him to fluff up that player and get him thinking straight again instead of being crushed by Lombardi's chew out. That was not the only time that happened. The year after I left, Pat Summerall came to the Giants from the Cardinals. In his book, Summerall talked about how Lombardi would put that pressure on him, and then Landry would help soothe him. It took both of them to make Summerall the great player that he became.

Tom Landry was a Texan and had played college ball at the University of Texas, but by the time I arrived he had played for the Giants for several years. He played up to that year, 1957, and was a full-time coach from that point on.

Since my dad was a preacher, and I grew up in the church, having someone like Tom Landry there really helped. Landry gave Bible studies to the players. He wanted everyone to have a solid foundation in the game of life as much as he wanted them to have a solid foundation playing football. He talked a lot about attitudes, families, and going to church. He believed in God first, family next, and then football. Of course, his coaching style was so intense on the practice field that I wondered a time or two if he had a short memory, because it seemed like he forgot the order of his beliefs.

Landry was probably the most perfect man that I've ever met. I mean that from a Christian standpoint. When he was in charge, we always had a prayer before workouts and a prayer before the game inside the dressing room—just the players. When someone was injured, Landry prayed over that player for his health and for his family. Landry was probably a little harder to get to really know because he was quiet and reserved, but he was just a jewel of a man.

Lombardi was a jewel of a man too, even though he could be tough and mean to his own players and to anyone else who was around. He showed me that he had a heart when he bought me that plane ticket to fly home to see my newborn baby daughter. I would have expected Landry to do something like that before Lombardi.

You always knew where you stood with Lombardi, though; he was honest and straightforward, and he did not beat around the bush. Lombardi's directness really didn't bother me because I was going to hustle anyway, and I was going to get better.

All of the coaches I played for had the same philosophy about being on time to team meetings. With Lombardi, the veterans had to be there at least thirty minutes before the meeting started. Rookies like me had to be there an hour early. That's always stuck with me. I never wanted to be late to anything after that.

CHAPTER THREE

FROM PLAYING
TO COACHING

Carole brought Chuck to church with her and after one Sunday morning worship service, in the foyer of the church, and knowing my background in athletics, Coach Curtis said to me, "That was an all-Southwest Conference sermon." That was the first time I had ever met him, though I was very much aware of his athletic successes as a player for TCU and as a state championship football coach at Jacksboro and Garland. I knew that he had been an assistant coach at SMU.

You can imagine how Chuck Curtis's statement made me feel. It is one of the most memorable and most appreciated comments I've ever had regarding my preaching, and of course, preachers are sensitive about their preaching. I had been a grader of sermons for the preaching professor course at Southwestern Baptist Theological Seminary, and I had been affirmed with the high honor of being selected as an alternate preacher for senior preaching week my last year at Southwestern but Coach Curtis's comment to me that day after church still sticks in my mind as a great encouragement to me personally. Then, the next Sunday, Coach Curtis and Carole came to church again . . . and after church, in the foyer of the church, as they were leaving, Coach Curtis made a similar comment about the sermon.

I walked away both times understanding better how Coach Curtis was a master at encouragement. It gave me insight into understanding how, with similar encouragement, he must have gotten the best out of his high school football players that led to three consecutive state championships. Had he accepted the head coaching job at Odessa Permian, he probably would have won a fourth straight state football championship—he is a master encourager. He knows where to "scratch you" to get the best out of you. I imagine that he got the absolute best out of those players he coached. He made them believe in themselves and made them never want to disappoint him. He made me also want to make sure that when I preached with Chuck Curtis in the congregation, even though my Master evaluator of sermons would be my Lord, every sermon would be an "all-Southwest Conference sermon."

REVEREND MARK BUMPUS, *Chuck and Carole's pastor at First Baptist Church in Mineral Wells, 1994-2008*

A t the end of the 1957 season, I thought, now is my chance to get into coaching. I got the playbooks of some of the greatest coaches. There's no way you can get that kind of help from clinics. I told the Giants I wanted to go into coaching. I could have played another year, because they extended my contract, but I decided to go into coaching instead.

I pretty well knew I wanted to coach after playing for Abe Martin at TCU. I liked his philosophy. We all wanted to win for Coach Martin, especially in the Greenbelt Bowl when he and Sammy Baugh were the coaches.

When I coached, I used a lot of Abe Martin's old sayings, and he had a lot of clever ones. Once he was talking to us quarterbacks, and he looked up from the film and said, referring to one of the receivers that we had somehow missed in the game, "He's as open as a butcher knife."

I started watching Coach Martin and all the assistant coaches when I was at TCU. When I was with the Giants, I had my own black book of all the plays and formations that Coach Lombardi had put in, and then whenever I could get into a defensive meeting I was also writing down Tom Landry's defensive alignments and responsibilities and how the shifts worked.

When I played for Winnipeg, I didn't know anybody in town, so all my time was spent studying offenses and defenses. When I was in New York, it was about the same. A few of the older players who had been there several years had apartments, but the rest of us stayed in the Concourse Plaza Hotel in the Bronx. For the most part I stayed in my hotel room after workouts and studied what we'd covered.

I've borrowed something from every one of my coaches. The multiple offense that I used in my coaching career started with my coach at Gainesville High. We ran about every type of formation you could think of, and we got to where we could run them all really well. Back then, everybody thought you needed to be one-dimensional in high school football, but at Gainesville we were not, and neither were any of the teams I coached.

Paul Brown, whom I played for in the Senior Bowl, was a brilliant guy. One thing he did was he shuttled the guards onto the field with plays instead of using signals from the sideline. So when I went into coaching, I started out calling the plays and shuttling my guards like Coach Brown did. Later in my career, I kept doing that, but I would use only the positions that had two players with equal ability so I wouldn't weaken the team by substituting in a lesser player.

My first coaching job, at age twenty-three in 1958, was at Holliday High School, a Class A school near Wichita Falls. I found out about the Holliday job from my wife's parents, who lived there and worked in the oil fields. They heard about the local high school coach leaving, and they told me about the opening at Holliday in the middle of the summer. I visited with the superintendent, W. A. Thomas, and I told him where I'd just been and who I'd played for, and he offered me the job on the spot.

I asked Dr. Thomas about the assistant coaches at Holliday. There were two coaches, and Dr. Thomas told me they coached all the sports at the junior high and high school levels, in addition to driving the bus and teaching classes.

I decided to accept the job offer, but on one condition. I told Dr. Thomas, "Before I take this job, I'm going to go and visit with them and make dang sure they're staying here if they're doing all that. Because I'll tell you, I can't do all that and come out of here with a winner."

We had some outstanding players at Holliday. I had an excellent quarterback, Merle Boyd. In addition to being a fine football player, he was great in track, hurdles, and basketball. Everything fell into place for us at Holliday that year. We won eight and lost two, barely missing the playoffs. Back then, only the district

Chuck and his assistant coaches, Dan Owen and Allen Gibbs, at Jacksboro High School. *Courtesy Jacksboro High School.*

champion could represent the district in the playoffs. If you finished second or lower, you went home. Even though we didn't qualify for the playoffs, we still had a great season.

In the eighth week, we played Iowa Park. The coach who had been at Holliday before me had left that job to go to Iowa Park, and the word that got around was that he left Holliday to go over there because he thought they had better players and a better chance to win. We used that information to motivate our players in the week leading up to the game, and we kicked his tail. We won that game 20-8.

Even though we had an outstanding year at Holliday, I moved on after just one year. I received an offer I couldn't refuse—to be the head coach at Abe Martin's alma mater, Jacksboro High School, located in Jack County west of Fort Worth, and about an hour's drive southeast of Holliday.

Jacksboro had just had a 0-10 season in 1958, with Abe Martin's brother coaching there. When the season was over at Holliday, the Jacksboro people immediately drove up to meet me and said, "We want you to be our coach." I said, "Let's just get after it then." I had only rented a house in Holliday, so the move

Coach Curtis and his assistant, Dan Owen, far right, are giving instructions to Jacksboro's three cocaptains in 1959. From left, Eddie Bonner, Gary Robinson, and Butch Ellis. *Courtesy Jacksboro High School.*

to Jacksboro wasn't too complicated. Coach Martin's mom and dad still lived there. It was a happy, TCU-type of community, and they wanted a winner. I had a meeting with the school board, and I accepted the position and went to work.

In 1959, my first year at Jacksboro, we won two and lost eight, but that was two hundred percent better than they did the year before. In 1960 we won nine and lost one, and the following season we went 13-1.

In my third year, 1961, Jacksboro High School burned down. I think it was an electrical problem that started the fire. The school burning down was quite a shock to all of us. But it got rid of an old school building that was unsafe, and it was replaced with a new one. When the district received the insurance money, they did a fine job of putting together a new school. I never did hear anybody of importance within the school administration say that the school burning down was a blessing in disguise, but I've often thought it to myself, and I've started thinking it out loud now.

The local Baptist church served as a temporary school while the new building was being constructed. That was a little different. It made us all try to be a little nicer and cleaner. The only real

In the fall of 1960, the Jacksboro Tigers won nine games and lost only one in their second year under the direction of Coach Curtis. *Courtesy Jacksboro High School.*

hardship on the football team was finding a place to dress and get our pads on. I think we used one of the other churches to get that done in order to save time. The new school was ready by the fall of 1962.

In 1962, four years after Jacksboro's 0-10 season, the team went 15-0. I don't know if the Jacksboro players ever had anybody come in and tell them what I told them, which was, "We will win the state championship if I can have all of you. And what I mean by all of you is your eyes, your ears, and doing it the way we tell you to do it. Then we're going to be able to enjoy what we have accomplished together. All of us, you and me. Us. Our assistant coaches are going to work you hard, and I'm going to work you hard. You're going to be in condition. You'll have fun because we are going to win. If I get all of you, we'll have a state championship thrown in there, too."

We had our kids in great condition, and we kept them in great condition. Many of them played both offense and defense. We got through the season without any injuries to the major players,

Jacksboro's coaching staff in the fall of 1961 consisted of, from left: Chuck Curtis, Dan Owen, and Allan Gibbs. *Courtesy Jacksboro High School.*

and everything just fell into place. That was the year we won the school's first title in football—the 1962 Class 2A state championship.

It was a major thrill to go from a 0-10 record to being undefeated state champions in four years. In '62, we scored more points than any other team in the state of Texas. We scored six hundred and two points and allowed only forty-two, and shut out eleven of the fifteen teams we played. We were the only undefeated and untied team that year in Texas. Some major things happened in Jacksboro that year, and I give the good Lord all the credit from my end.

Steve Wheelis, our quarterback, helped lead us to an undefeated, untied season in 1962. We won the '62 state championship game, 52-0, over Rockdale, and Steve was responsible for forty-four of the fifty-two points. His older brother David was a quarterback for me at Jacksboro, too. He was a senior while Steve was a sophomore. Their dad was a doctor, and both their parents were big golfers, so both Steve and David were influenced by the example of their parents.

Steve was something else. He was probably the best athlete I ever coached. He was a tall, lanky kid and a really great passer. A really pure passer. He also played defense for us in the secondary, and he had a knack for getting to the ball. He had a lot of interceptions for us. He had height, and he could really read opposing offenses and go get the ball. He could do it all—he could throw, punt, kick, and play safety.

He could play golf, too. In addition to coaching football, I was the golf coach at Jacksboro. We won the state championship in golf in the spring of 1963, and Steve Wheelis was the golfer who won it for us. With a winning football team and a golf team that won the state championship, Jacksboro dominated Class 2A sports in Texas that year.

After high school, Steve was offered a scholarship to TCU, and Abe Martin told him he could play golf or football. He played football the first year and played golf for the rest of his time in college.

I didn't know it at the time, but the 1962 football season was to be my last at Jacksboro High School for seventeen years. During our state championship run that year the Jacksboro Tigers played Mineola, a school about eighty miles east of Dallas, in the state quarterfinal playoff game. We played them at Williams Stadium in Garland, a halfway point between Jacksboro and Mineola.

The athletic director for the Garland ISD and head football coach at Garland High School was Homer B. Johnson, and he told my Jacksboro team and me to just come on down. The folks at the Garland ISD really took care of us. We beat Mineola, 40-0, in Garland, and then won the next two games to win the state title.

I had no idea Homer had been watching me and all of the playoff games Jacksboro played that year. Nor did I know he was about to step aside as head football coach of Garland High School. Garland was scheduled to open a second high school—South Garland High School—in 1964, and Homer would become a full-time athletic director for the school district. He could have stayed on at Garland as the coach, but he said, "If I do, they'll just hire someone to be my boss." So he took the athletic director job.

After the 1962 football season was over, I got a phone call from Homer. He told me that Garland was going to have a school board meeting, and that he'd like me to come down for it. He wanted me to interview for the head football coach position at Garland High School, if I was interested. I had been at Jacksboro for four years, and I was ready to move to a larger school. The Garland Owls had a bit of a football history, since they had won the 3A state championship a few years earlier in 1956, when Homer was an assistant coach. Now Garland was 4A.

I told Homer, "Yes, sir, I'm interested in the job, and I'll be there for the interview." I went to Garland to meet with the school board. After we had an interview, I went out for a cup of coffee while they convened. I didn't know it at the time, but the board wanted to hire another coach, and Homer wanted to hire me. This caused a commotion at the meeting, so when Homer came out of it he announced, "I have good news and bad news. Which do you want first?"

I answered, "I want the good news first."

He said, "You're hired."

So I asked, "What's the bad news?"

He replied, "If you don't win, they're going to fire both of us."

It worked out great for both of us. We won the 4A state championship both years I was at Garland, and we had an overall record of 26-1-1. Homer kept his job, and in fact he's kept it for more than fifty years. And the school board in Garland has let him hire every head football coach in the district since then.

When I started at Garland in 1963, I was only twenty-eight years old. I must have been the youngest head coach in 4A Texas football at the time. Homer was loyal and a strong backer for a young coach who was really pressing all the buttons and overworking his kids. He did a great job of keeping us all in line and feeling positive, and that's a big reason we were so successful. We had some fun along the way. We did have to correct the kids at times, but it was never anything serious.

Homer reminded me a lot of Abe Martin. I liked his sense

Garland players carry Coach Curtis off the field after a
playoff win in 1963. *Courtesy Garland High School.*

of humor. I really liked him, and I really wanted to win for him. It didn't matter whether you were a millionaire or a homeless person; Homer treated everybody the same, and that was what I enjoyed about him. He really worked hard to help us achieve success at Garland. I thought he did a spectacular job of getting us what we needed. We were able to go to the games in first-class style. For the state championship game in 1964, we flew in a Braniff Airlines jet from Dallas to Houston. I don't know of any other high school football teams that traveled by airplane back then.

Homer was the best athletic director I ever had. He was the only athletic director I've ever had at the high school level. At all of the other high schools where I coached, I was the head football coach and athletic director. Garland was the first place where I was just the football coach, and I loved every minute of it.

I learned a lot from Homer. I really love that man and what he's done for Garland and for high school sports in general in more than fifty years that he's been an athletic director. I'm appreciative of everything he did for me when I was coaching at Garland High School. He's been such an inspiration and a positive influence on thousands of kids and coaches over the decades. His tenure with the Garland ISD has to be some kind of record for coaches. He began as an assistant coach at Garland High School in 1948, so 2014 is his sixty-sixth year with the school district.

Chuck Curtis with his former coaching colleagues at a Garland High School reunion in 2010. From left, Homer B. Johnson, Merle Boyd, Chuck, R.E. Dodson, and Ernie Cunningham. *Photo courtesy Steve Rhodes.*

Homer let me pick my assistant coaches at Garland. I hired two former TCU players as my assistant coaches for my first year at Garland High School, O'Day Williams and R.E. Dodson. O'Day had been my teammate when we beat Jim Brown and Syracuse in the Cotton Bowl. My defensive coordinator, Ernie Cunningham, was from Midwestern University.

I had a hard decision to make that first year. I was in a position to recommend someone for head coach at the new high school in town. For me, it fell back to the fact that O'Day Williams was the first coach I hired at Garland. There were some others on my staff I thought could do well also, but since O'Day was my first hire, I gave him the first shot, and he went for it. So in 1964 O'Day left to become the first-ever head coach at South Garland. We replaced him on my Garland staff with another TCU alum, Bill Yung.

Don Schmidt was on our staff at Garland, and he was a Texas Tech boy. When I first hired him, I went to a game or two with him to scout our upcoming opponents. We were in the stands watching the action on the field, and I saw that he had an exceptional eye for scouting, remembering, and putting things down

The Garland High School coaching staff in 1963, Chuck's first year at the school: clockwise from top left, Ernie Cunningham, R.E. Dodson, O'Day Williams, and Coach Curtis. *Courtesy Garland High School.*

on paper. Because of that, I made him my head scout. Usually he would catch not only one game ahead of us, but two. Sometimes he would be three games ahead if they were playing close enough together. The information he brought back was a big factor in our winning seasons.

I probably had one of the best coaching staffs at any high school anywhere. Not only were they outstanding football players, they were also close friends of mine and wonderful people. You've got to be good friends with your coaches because you spend lots of hours working together. You receive the benefits and joys of success on game night after you win, but getting there is a lot of work, and that's why I chose the people that I did. They lived the right type of life to be examples, and they fit right in.

I was a little disappointed when I first saw the Garland kids. My Jacksboro players were a little larger man-for-man than the ones at Garland. But what I liked that changed my mind immediately was Garland's quickness and speed. Also, Garland's skill players could catch, and they could run. There were two or three off the track team that really helped us out. We utilized speed instead of worrying so much about brute strength. I told the kids, "I've got the formula. I've got the best plays of the teams I've been with in college and high school. If you all will give me all you've got, that's all I want. We'll win a state championship here. Everybody wants to win. The difference is not everybody wants to pay the price. You have to want to pay the price, and you have to do it team-wise, not individually."

Their eyes got big when I told them I had the formula for winning the state championship. The Garland players knew I had just won a state championship with Jacksboro and had won it in big fashion by beating Rockdale, 52-0. The teaching end of it fell right in. I told them at the beginning of the season in 1963, "We'll have lots of celebrations down the road if we'll make the sacrifice now to be the smartest football players we can be and be as quick and as strong as we can between now and then."

We showed them the difference between winning and losing. I didn't have to do much more preaching than that. They believed in my game plan, and they were willing to try my philosophy.

We got the Garland players in condition by running two-hundred-and-twenty-yard sprints and running up and down the bleachers at the Williams Stadium. We didn't have weights back then, but we had a couple of parallel bars across there. I'd have the team "walk" along them with their hands holding their bodies up, to get strength in the shoulders and give the legs a rest, too. They would really work, not just physically, but mentally. They prepared themselves with scouting reports, and our game plan fell right in. We ran our plays over and over and over again in practice. We made sure everybody knew what to do in certain situations. They kept practice fun, even though it was hard work, and they were repaid tenfold for the extra thinking and for being smart.

Chuck as the head coach of the
Garland Owls in 1963.
Courtesy Garland High School.

Coach Curtis surveys Garland's
situation from the sidelines.
Courtesy Garland High School.

The results on the field for Garland in 1963 were pretty much the same as my team had at Jacksboro the year before. We scored three hundred and eighty-five points in fourteen games and allowed only ninety-three points, with five shutouts.

We beat our big district rival, Highland Park, 22-20 at their place in the fifth week of the season. We had to come from behind in the fourth quarter to do it. Garland had never beaten Highland Park before that. It was one of those games that could have gone either way, but I think we wanted it a little more than they did.

We started the fourth quarter down, 14-7. We got the ball and started moving it, and we got down inside the ten-yard line where we were able to work it on in with just under eight minutes left to play. I had called a jump pass to my big old tight end, Lowell Halpin. I called him "Ichabod" after Ichabod Crane because he had such big feet. Our quarterback, Jimmy Adams, was to fake the ball to the fullback and then make a jump pass to Halpin. Well, I don't know if Highland Park knew for sure what we were doing, but they read it pretty well. After the snap of the

Chuck and Carole share memories with former Garland High School quarterback Jimmy Adams and his wife, Vicki, during a trip back to Garland in 2010. *Photo courtesy Steve Rhodes.*

ball, the first thing I saw was that Halpin was knocked down by a linebacker and another defender right at the feet of Adams, who was just getting ready to throw. The first thing that went through my mind is that Jimmy could easily complete that pass, because Halpin was right there at his toes. But a situation like that is no time to be working on your percentiles. After faking the pass, Jimbo wheeled on around to the outside and handed off to Gary Bridges, who ran it in fifteen yards for the touchdown. We trailed by just one, 14-13, at that point.

Then we had to make a big decision. Do we go for a two-point conversion and the lead or go for one and a tie? I looked back at our entire crowd, and we all decided to go for two. On the next play, one of our halfbacks, Bill Crump, slid out into the flat. We were bringing a split end back to the inside, and he sealed off the defender that was fixin' to try and make the tackle. Crump caught it and just went on in, giving us a one-point edge. Later we scored another touchdown on a run by Ralph Weaver, and an extra point by Chris Sims, to take a 22-14 lead with just

The *Garland Daily News* captured it when Texas Longhorns coach Darrell Royal, at the podium, made a presentation to Coach Curtis, at far left, and the Garland High School football players at a Lions Club football banquet in 1964. *Courtesy Garland News.*

under three minutes left. Highland Park got the ball back and drove for a touchdown with time running out, but we stopped them on the two-point attempt and came away with a 22-20 win. After the game was over, while I was still on the field, the Garland fans came pouring out onto the grass. All the excited mommas and pappies were swarming us. The field was just covered with fans. We had finally beaten Highland Park.

I looked at my watch and thought, "My players are already in the dressing room." I didn't see any more players out on the field. It was just moms and dads a-huggin' and a-kissin' each other.

When I made it to the dressing room and opened the door, there was a quiet like I've never felt before in a dressing room. I looked over to the right, and the big linemen had their heads bowed, praying. The receivers on the next row over were praying. I looked back around to my captains. Ralph Weaver, our fullback, was the one who eased up to me and said, "Coach, would you lead us in a word of prayer?"

And that's what I did.

From that point forward, no matter what team I was coaching, we always prayed as a team in the locker room after a game. Sometimes I would lead the prayer and sometimes I would ask my players if one of them felt inspired to lead the prayer. But since my Garland team beat Highland Park in 1963, and we prayed together as a team after the game, it was that way from that point on.

When we beat Highland Park for the first time ever, we accomplished another mission: we came together as a team. That win really got us started and removed all doubts about whether or not we were a top-notch football team. At that point, we knew we were, and it looked like some happy days were ahead.

And they were, because later that year, we played Miller High School from Corpus Christi for the 4A state championship in Austin, and we beat them 17-0, for a 13-0-1 season.

We played that game at Memorial Stadium on the campus of the University of Texas. Our kids enjoyed playing in Austin and seeing coaching legend Darrell Royal. Our fullback, Ralph Weaver, played an outstanding game for us on both offense and defense, and he was named MVP of the game. He made a lot of tough yardage for us on offense.

Miller had some excellent skill players in the secondary, so we held Jimmy Adams back a little bit at first. We were trying to avoid the interception by going for the easy passes. As the game progressed, with Weaver running so well, they focused on trying to stop him. Then we got to work on our passing game, and Jim completed several more difficult passes.

We dominated in '64 just like we did in '63, except for one game. Highland Park beat us in week seven, 20-14. We needed a wakeup call. It turned out to be the only game Garland lost in the two years that I coached there. That loss really ticked us off, because Garland players were not used to losing. I know this—we didn't have to holler much louder when we started working out to get ready for the next game, because the players were just as sick about losing as we were, and they knew we could do better. They played a good game against Highland Park but knew it wasn't their best. In the games before and after that one, my players had a clear mind, and they played at their best.

One player who was at his best in a 1964 playoff game was our quarterback, Jimmy Adams. He was one of the most competitive players I ever coached. He was extremely confident. He blended right in with our team's personality and our philosophy of trying to stay positive all the time in our coaching methods. He fell right in there, preaching the same gospel as we did. For a first-year quarterback as a junior in 1963, he was outstanding.

Jimmy had one of his best games in the bidistrict playoff game in 1964 against Texas High from Texarkana. We had played them in that same round of the playoffs in 1963 at our place, and blew them out, 58-14. The '64 game was at Texarkana, and their coach was really mad at us for what we did the year before. Late in the game, they had us in big trouble, because they were ahead, 16-13, and they were driving deep in our territory. Our linebacker, Gene Mayes, who went on to play football at TCU, made four tackles in a row, and they turned it over on downs. We got the ball on our one-yard line with just over two minutes to play.

Jimmy was confident in the huddle even though he needed to gain 99 yards in two minutes with no timeouts. He proclaimed to his teammates, "Never fear, Jimbo's here!" Then he marched the team right down the field. Jimmy's first pass was to Ron Scoggins. He had the option of running his slant to the inside at an angle, or running it wide to the outside. I figured he'd take it wide to the outside. He made a fake like he was going to the outside, but then he turned back up field. Jimbo read Ron just right and hit him with a perfect pass.

Four times in that march, we faced a fourth down. And four times we ended up making a first down. That's the kind of team it was—our players stayed positive all the time. Scoggins scored the winning touchdown with thirty-six seconds left. Garland won that playoff game, 20-16, and won the next two games to take on Galena Park for the state championship at Rice Stadium in Houston.

Galena Park had been to the 4A state championship game two years earlier, but lost to Wichita Falls. When we played for

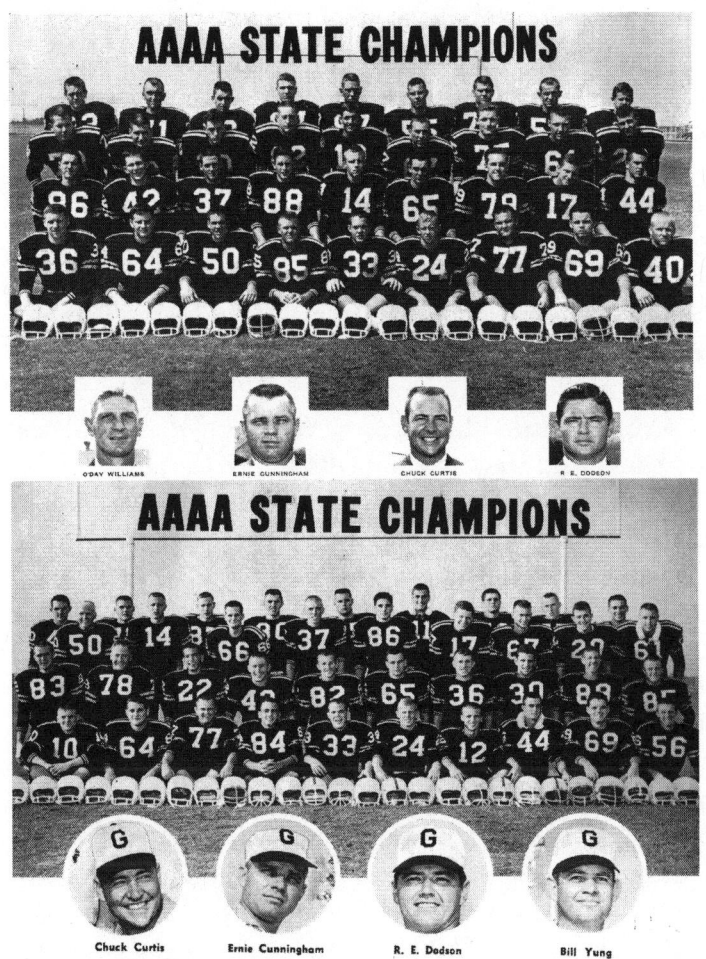

AAAA STATE CHAMPIONS

O'DAY WILLIAMS   ERNIE CUNNINGHAM   CHUCK CURTIS   R. E. DODSON

AAAA STATE CHAMPIONS

Chuck Curtis   Ernie Cunningham   R. E. Dodson   Bill Yung

The Garland Owls were back-to-back Texas Class 4A state champions in 1963 and 1964 under the coaching of Chuck Curtis and his staff. *Courtesy Garland High School.*

the 4A state title in '64, Galena Park got out to a 14-0 lead on us. For their first touchdown, they threw a bounced pass to the wide receiver. The receiver was back behind the line of scrimmage so that the pass would be a lateral. And of course, a lateral that hits the ground is a live ball. Their quarterback threw it to the ground just in front of the wide receiver, and they had worked on it enough to where it popped up right in front of him. We knew that, but yet we didn't stop it the first time. We pulled up, thinking it was an incomplete pass, and that receiver took off like a scalded dog. That got our attention. It was a called play they had really worked on, and they caught us flat footed. From thenceforth and thereafter, we played to the rules a little better.

Fortunately, we had enough time to come back. We had one half to beat them, and that was all we needed. We started running our fullback, Clifton Turner, and we were faking to one of the speedy halfbacks and then going right down the line and handing off to Turner. Their big defensive tackles took the bait every time we faked to the halfback running behind the guard. He'd come on down and hit that halfback, but it was Turner, the fullback, who had the ball on the outside of him. Turner had the most yardage that night, too, and he was named the MVP.

The play where we used to give it to Turner was a lot like the belly series except we didn't ride the halfback. The belly series was our biggest play when I played at TCU. We had a big old tough fullback, and I'd take the ball and actually put it in his belly and ride him up into the line and pull it back, then work on down the line of scrimmage and hand it to the halfback that was coming around. The idea was to fake the defense out and make them think that the fullback had the ball. We could also pass using this play if for some reason we didn't fake out the defense.

The belly series was big-time football in those early years. Football teams don't use it much any more, since everyone's gone to the wide-open spread. Athletes now can throw better and catch better. They're faster and they're more educated about the game. We barely had TV back then, so my contemporaries and I really learned from scratch. I took the belly series with me from TCU, and there might have been one or two more schools that ran it, but it was our bread and butter at Garland.

If I had stayed at Garland for a third year, I believe it would have been just like the first two years. I think we could have won the state championship again. I would have kept doing the same thing, because what we were doing was working.

After we won the state championship with Garland in 1964, I moved on to become an assistant coach at Southern Methodist

University in Dallas under head coach Hayden Fry, who later became well known for coaching at Iowa. I also received an offer to be the head coach at Odessa Permian High School, a 4A school in West Texas. Permian became famous in the early '90s for the book *Friday Night Lights* and for winning several state championships over the years, but it was a fairly new school in 1964 when I interviewed for the job. Permian won the first of many state championships in 1965. It makes me wonder if I'd taken the job, could I have won four straight state championships at three different schools? We'll never know.

When I look back, I wish I had taken the Odessa Permian job. After I interviewed for it, I was pretty sure I would take it. But I also wanted to get into college coaching as soon as I could. When I got back home to Dallas, I got the offer to go to SMU, and I thought, "I might not get another chance to get into college coaching. I'm here, in an area that I'm familiar with, so the time is right for me to make the move from high school to college."

Sometimes things weren't too smooth between Coach Fry and me, because we each wanted to do it our own way. I was used to being in charge. I called all the plays when I was the quarterback at TCU. I had always been the head coach at Holliday, Jacksboro, and Garland, and I had never been an assistant coach. At SMU, I did most of my coaching during the week, working with the quarterbacks and getting them all ready for that Saturday's game. I got to call a few plays at particular times if I knew something was going to work. But it was still Fry's ballgame, so I stayed out of the way as far as that went. I didn't want to do anything stupid to force the team to choose either me or him.

One thing about the SMU job I really enjoyed was recruiting. In 1965, I recruited Jerry LeVias, the first African American scholarship athlete in the Southwest Conference, to play for SMU. I didn't set out to break the so-called "color barrier," I just walked into the situation, and I was in the right place at the right time. I was supposed to find the best athletes, and Jerry was the best athlete I found.

I was able to find Jerry LeVias because my recruiting area was all of Texas. I arrived at SMU too late for me to have a recruiting territory, so Coach Fry just told me to circle the whole state and find the best athletes. I just hit all the high spots. I kept hearing more about Jerry as I got closer to the Beaumont area east of Houston and close to the Texas-Louisiana border. I knew he had already won the state championship in sprinting at Hebert High School in Beaumont. He was a basketball player, and at 5-foot-9 he could dunk the basketball while standing flat footed underneath the basket. I watched him in PE class catch the football and tuck it away and go. I couldn't believe my eyes.

I knew Jerry would be the perfect fit for us at SMU. When I started checking his character and his grades, and then I met his momma and daddy, I discovered what an outstanding overall young man he was. They knew we'd take care of him. And his momma was a wonderful cook, so I didn't mind going to Beaumont to stay with his family.

My first assignments were to take Jerry to all the high school football all-star games. The first one was the Big 33 game in Hershey, Pennsylvania, which was the Texas high school all-stars against the Pennsylvania all-stars. Coach Fry said, "I want you to take him, and I want you to bring him back. Don't let anyone else steal him from us." I responded, "It shall be done."

Jerry ended up being named the most valuable player of the Big 33 game. He ran back a kickoff, ran back a punt, and caught a touchdown pass. After the game, Tommy Prothro, the UCLA coach, tried to steal him from me. Tommy and I had a little scuffle, but I won that one. It made the headlines up there in Pennsylvania and in Dallas, too. I thought, "I haven't even made it to the season yet, and I'm probably going to get fired with this type of negative publicity."

I didn't get fired, though. I brought Jerry back to Texas just in time to play in the 1965 Oil Bowl game in Wichita Falls, where it was the Texas all-stars against Oklahoma all-stars. He was named the most valuable player again as the Texas all-stars won, 21-13. Jerry was named to the Oil Bowl Hall of Fame in 2006 for his performance in that game.

We had us something special with Jerry LeVias. He just did wonders for us when he started working out with the team. We tried to groom him to get him to where he could play on the varsity for SMU the same way he played in the Oil Bowl and the Big 33 game, and he did, starting the following year in 1966. He was also a model student off the field. He was a brilliant kid.

Jerry did encounter some racism from the teams we played and the fans of those teams, and when he did, he handled it well. He had people hollering nasty things at him here and there, but he stayed above them. I was working on the sidelines during the ballgames, trying to keep him feeling good. Right before one game, Coach Fry came over to me and informed me, "I'd rather have you in the press box today." I said, "Ok, but I'd rather be on the sideline. I'd feel more comfortable there." He responded, "You see those men behind us with the sun shades on? They're from the FBI. You've had a death threat. Whoever made the threat may not be as good a shot as they think they are, and most of the time you're standing next to me, so I think you ought to go up to the press box." That was all he needed to say to convince me. I told Coach Fry, "I don't need an elevator." So I went on up to the press box. Thankfully, we ended up not having any trouble.

When we got Jerry LeVias, he was the last skill player we really needed. He was our lifesaver. In 1966, his first year on varsity, he helped us beat A&M, Texas, Baylor, and TCU, all toughies in the Southwest Conference. When we beat the Aggies, 21-14, in the seventh game of the season on November 5, Gene Stallings, who was then the coach at A&M, said, "We didn't get beat by SMU. We got beat by an all-United Nations team," because Jerry LeVias caught the winning touchdown pass from Ines Perez, who was our quarterback.

Jerry LeVias became a star receiver, and SMU won the conference championship for the first time in eighteen years in 1966. We lost only two games during the regular season, to Purdue and Arkansas, and we earned a bid to the Cotton Bowl where we lost to Georgia, 24-9.

When he was a senior, and after I had left SMU, Jerry was named all-American as he led the Mustangs to an 8-3 record and a 28-27 victory over the University of Oklahoma in the 1968

Chuck Curtis spent two years (1965-66)
as an assistant coach at SMU.
Courtesy SMU.

Bluebonnet Bowl in Houston. He went on to play for the Houston Oilers and the San Diego Chargers in the NFL. Later he was inducted into the Texas Sports Hall of Fame and the national College Football Hall of Fame.

Jerry's coach for his last year with the Chargers in 1974 was none other than Tommy Prothro. So Tommy eventually got him, but not before he had completed a hall of fame career with us at SMU.

My tenure at SMU lasted just two years, the 1965 and 1966 seasons. It was the goal of the people who hired me at SMU for me to become the head coach there within a year or two. Coach Fry had been there several years by that time, and the team hadn't been too successful. After we won the Southwest Conference in 1966, they gave Coach Fry an extension, so he wasn't going anywhere for a while (he stayed on at SMU until 1972). But I got just as much out of it, and more, maybe, with the excitement of winning the Southwest Conference and the excitement of being able to recruit Jerry LeVias.

After the 1966 football season, I decided to get out of coaching altogether and started Chuck Curtis Ford, a car dealership in Terrell, east of Dallas. A lot of the people who supported me at Chuck Curtis Ford were SMU alumni. The dealership was quite a departure from being a football coach, but I had some experience selling cars at Dick Danner Ford in Fort Worth back when I was in college at TCU. With my experience and the backing we had, Chuck Curtis Ford took off and was highly successful.

I stayed with my car dealership for about two years, but then I started feeling like I hadn't quite gotten all the coaching out of me. One of Grand Prairie's school board members called me when they had an opening for head football coach at Grand Prairie High School. That changed my mind about the car dealership and got me thinking about coaching again. I had a chance to sell the car dealership, so I sold it and got back into coaching at Grand Prairie in time for the 1968 football season.

Since I went through junior high school in Grand Prairie, and my dad had been the pastor of the First Assembly of God Church there years earlier, I thought it would really be fun going back to my hometown. But it just didn't work out for me. It really turned out to be a mistake to coach there.

At first, the school board was going to enlarge Grand Prairie High and keep it a one-high-school town. But instead of doing that, they decided to build another high school in the south part of Grand Prairie. That diluted the football talent in the town, and a lot of our better players went over to the new high school.

Following this experience, I again lost my zeal for coaching. I left Grand Prairie after the 1969 football season, and at thirty-four years old I decided to go into banking full time.

Banking was not exactly new to me. While I was at SMU a few years earlier, I was able to take some courses at the Southwest Graduate School of Banking. That gave me enough background to get into banking.

My first job in banking was working for Lakewood Bank and Trust in the east part of Dallas. I was a vice president and did some business development. There were several Garland people that were on the board of directors there, and they had fond memories of me from my time coaching at Garland High School.

I really enjoyed banking. I played a lot of golf with the people who helped the bank the most.

I had some big-name people as customers at Lakewood Bank and Trust, like Mickey Mantle of the New York Yankees, Bob Lilly of TCU and the Dallas Cowboys, and a few others. They would bring some business with them, and they would always give autographs to customers at the bank.

Bob Lilly was from the West Texas town of Throckmorton. I was a senior at TCU while he was a freshman, and he was my freshman. Each one of us on varsity was responsible for grabbing a freshman and staying with him, keeping him going, and getting him to do a few things by way of initiation into the team. Lilly shined my boots for me when he was a freshman. A year or two later, I would not have asked him to do that.

Lilly is remembered as one of the best football players ever to play for TCU. He was an all-American, and later he made it into both the College and Pro Football Halls of Fame. He was a defensive star for Tom Landry and the Dallas Cowboys for many years. Lilly was pretty special, especially since it was a penny postcard that got him to come to TCU. That was a surprise. Coach Mac White, our line coach, sent Lilly a postcard asking him to come and take a look at us, and that's how Lilly came to TCU.

I had also known Mickey Mantle for many years by the late '60s, and we had become great friends. Mickey lived in Dallas, and he was really a Texan even though he was raised in Oklahoma.

He was an enjoyable guy, like an overgrown kid; he liked to have fun, and he could pretty much do anything he wanted. He liked to slip off and get out of the Dallas area now and then. He liked to play golf, and he liked to gamble on his golf game. He'd make bets with people on who could hit a golf ball the farthest. Then it got to where nobody would bet against him, because he could hit it into the day after tomorrow.

We did a lot of hunting and fishing together. Once we even bought an entire ranch not far from Jacksboro, just because Mickey liked the fishing there. We went out there to hunt some quail, because Mickey really liked shotgun shooting. When we were out there looking it over, we noticed there was a lake, and he said, "I wish I'd brought my fishing pole." I said, "We can go back to town and get it." So we went back to Jacksboro to the only hardware store in town. That hardware store had a Zebco fishing pole, and we bought it. When we got back to the lake, on the first cast Mickey threw out there, he reeled in a nice bass. He said, "Let's buy the ranch, because the fishing is worth it." Then we discovered it was a prime hunting spot, too. We saw a covey or two of quail while we were out there. Mickey didn't have his gun with him, but I had mine in my truck, so I let him use it. He was an excellent marksman, too. He killed about a half a dozen quail. Between the bass and the quail, that put the deal together. We bought the place, and we hunted and fished there consistently.

On one occasion, Mickey was scheduled to meet President Richard Nixon as part of the celebration of the one hundredth anniversary of Major League Baseball. Mickey called me and said he needed me to help him. He told me that he was going to the White House to meet the President, and he was taking his girlfriend. Mickey wanted me to claim his girlfriend as mine when the press was around. He made sure that I knew when the press or other people were not around, she was with him. That suited me just fine.

Mickey went on to say, "I got you an airline ticket, and we're going to Washington, and from there we're going to Florida."

So we went to the White House, and he had me go through security. I was acting just like I was a New York Yankee. Then we caught the next plane to Florida. That's when his country kitchen restaurant that was opening up went public. We had to go to finish that up in Florida, and then come back to Dallas. Mickey did play a round or two of golf when we were in Florida to satisfy some of the investors. The result of all that was I put an $800,000 check for a return on bank shares into my pocket from his restaurant going public. A lot of people bought in and invested just because it was Mickey's restaurant. When I got back to Dallas, I deposited the check at Lakewood Bank and Trust.

I won employee of the week that week.

I put a group together from Lakewood Bank and Trust, and we bought a little bank in Bryson, which is just west of Jacksboro. We bought that bank and put together another group and bought the Bank of Crowley, just south of Fort Worth. Mickey Mantle was on our board of directors to help put those transactions together. He was our name out front; he didn't know anything about banking, and he didn't have to as long as he played golf with the investors or did whatever he could to make them happy.

Around that time, the mid-1970s, I got big time—and probably bigger than I should have been—into the cattle and ranching business. Mickey Mantle was my partner. I was buying land and buying cattle, and I had cattle from Oklahoma all the way to New Mexico. I had connections in Canada from playing football there, and I used those connections to get cattle imported from France to Canada, and then into the United States, primarily to Texas.

Another one of my partners was Ralph Hall, who was a US Senator from Rockwall, east of Dallas. Ralph was an attorney, and he helped us quite a bit with technical wisdom. He also assisted in the political end of it by buying land and ranches, and getting financing and cattle. He helped us with everything that needed to be done.

The cattle brought in from France were called Maine-Anjou cattle. Those are the show cattle. To this day, cross-bred Maine-Anjou cattle are winning all the money. The first pair of Maine-Anjou cattle we brought in, a momma cow and her calf, fetched $35,000 for us, and it looked like there was never going to be another poor day. Before too long I was a millionaire, and the way things looked, I was going to be a multimillionaire. We even bought an airplane, and we'd fly to San Antonio if we wanted Mexican food for dinner.

In hindsight, moves like buying an airplane we didn't need were not smart financial decisions. We spent a little too much time enjoying ourselves when we should have been tending to business. That came back to haunt us when the market crashed.

At one point, I owned several thousand acres and had three

thousand head of cattle. While we were buying cattle and putting all that together, the prices started rising. But after we had a couple of successful years in the cattle business, the market started downward, and suddenly I couldn't sell the cattle fast enough to pay the bank. We were wheelin' and dealin' the Maine-Anjou cattle, but the other kinds of cattle were dropping in price every day. The price of real estate was dropping, too. The big savings and loan in Olney, Texas, where we were doing some business, went under. That's when we took a sure enough whipping. I was forced into bankruptcy and was trying to get the creditors to hold off on collecting from me. But the bank decided to go on with it.

Mickey Mantle got out of our business before the market crashed, and it turned out to be a wise move for him to get out at that time. Mickey wasn't interested in cattle. He knew nothing about livestock, and he didn't like riding horses. He just went in with us early, and he got out of the deal pretty soon after we were rolling in the money. We had bought the little ranch where he could fish and hunt. But he wanted out of the deal, so we let him out.

Six months after I went into bankruptcy, the market came back up. But I didn't have near the number of cattle left by then.

The bank in Oklahoma is the one that caused most of my problems. At the time I had cattle mortgaged at that bank. I got all the cattle in Oklahoma and New Mexico, and I was able to send a bunch of cattle out there. We sold those in California, so it was getting better. But I had cattle mortgaged at the Wichita Falls bank, too. I was selling the Wichita Falls cattle in Oklahoma and paying the Oklahoma bank, and the Wichita Falls bank caught on. They presented me with a Uniform Commercial Code-1 form, which is a banking item that states for sure what you're mortgaging. I had signed that UCC-1 form earlier, but I didn't read it closely enough when I signed it. The fine print said, "All cattle now owned or hereafter acquired and the increase thereafter is put into the undersigned's note at the bank." I had mortgaged the type of cattle I had owned with the Wichita Falls bank, and I was selling them in Oklahoma. So technically, I was breaking the law. I kept selling those cattle in Oklahoma and pay-

Chuck and his daughter, Kim, enjoy a trail ride together in the mid-1990s.

ing off the Wichita Falls bank, and I finally got them paid off, but the Wichita Falls bank busted me for violating the UCC. I had to pay a $500 fine because of a technicality.

When my cattle business got too big, and I was trying to get everybody paid off, things got so bad that I started thinking that suicide was the easiest way out. My credit was ruined and I had no money. I had no job, and I was divorced from my first wife, Sue, around that time. Everything just fell apart. I wasn't living right. I was drinking, slipping back into sin, and doing a lot of bad things. I was making shady business deals if I could make them. I never gave thanks to God like I should have while my business was successful. The devil was talking to me too much, and unfortunately I listened. I wasn't listening to the good Lord.

If I'd been living right, I don't think I would have lost every-thing. It took all that getting taken away for me to realize what I was doing and turn things around. It also took some divine intervention with the help of my daughter, Kim, to keep me from ending my life.

❶ Kim was a teenager at that time. I had taken a trip up to Oklahoma to sell some cattle I had up there, and I was staying at a Holiday Inn in Ardmore, not too far from the Oklahoma-Texas border. I was working day and night trying to repay some loans.

I had a few drinks in the bar that night before I went back to my room. I had a gun with me, and I thought about just ending it right then and there.

I was about to go through with it when all of a sudden there was a knock on the door, and it was Kim. She brought her Bible and put it down and said, "I thought you might need to do some reading." We did some reading from the Bible in the book of Job, Chapter 22, verse 21: "Yield now and be at peace with Him; Thereby, God will come to you." I was hurriedly trying to get spiritually fed. When we finished reading, we prayed together. I didn't share it with her right then, but later I told her what she saved me from doing.

It was a miracle that Kim found me. She made the forty-mile trip from Gainesville, Texas, where she lived at the time, across the Oklahoma border to Ardmore, and the number two hundred and twenty-five was stuck in her head. That turned out to be my room number. She had to have been directed from above, because she had no idea where I was. I could have been in Oklahoma or in New Mexico or any one of a jillion places, but she managed to find me.

From that point on, I was serious about trying to get my life back on track and including God in my thoughts. Thereafter, at times I slid back a notch or two, but it seemed like I always came back stronger and made fewer mistakes.

Kim has always been a blessing to me. She went to the University of Texas, so I had to forgive her for going to one of TCU's biggest rivals. After she graduated from college, she went to work teaching fifth grade in Cleburne, Texas, which is about thirty miles south of Fort Worth. She started teaching in Cleburne around the same time that I became head football coach there in 1981. She still teaches fifth grade in Cleburne to this day.

Not too long after Kim found me at the Holiday Inn, I started putting my priorities in the correct order. The first thing I did was try to figure out what business I could make the most money in, the quickest, to make sure I got everybody paid off. I had sold sporting goods years earlier when I coached at Garland. I decided to go back into the sporting goods business.

I had lots of friends in Jacksboro that stayed with me through thick and thin. I had a nice place that I built there, outside of town. My folks were getting old, so I had a house on the ranch for them, too. I had a base to operate from, and I was ready to really push sporting goods.

I covered nine states, selling almost every brand of equipment. The coaches that I knew and made friends with over the years stayed with me. By this time, around 1979, Hayden Fry was at Iowa, and he bought equipment from me. Everyone thought we were enemies from my time coaching with him at SMU, but we really weren't. We got along probably better than everybody figured we did. Before I came to SMU in 1965, he was fixin' to get fired, and then I came and we recruited Jerry LeVias. With LeVias on board, we won the Southwest Conference, and then Fry received a big contract extension.

All the other coaches that I had made contact with over the years bought from me, too. I was selling primarily wholesale to the sporting goods stores that were spread out all over the country, and I would spend time with the closest university and offer deals on shoes, or uniforms, or whatever. That got me back in the fast lane and back into sports.

It took a few years, but I eventually got everyone paid off. At that point I got out of sporting goods and got back into doing what I was happiest doing, which was coaching.

It started when I received a phone call from a school board member in Jacksboro in 1979. The board member asked me what I had the most fun doing out of all the things I'd done. I told him it was coaching, and he informed me they had a head football coach opening at Jacksboro, and he offered me the job. I accepted immediately and went back to work at the school where I had won my first state championship back in 1962.

Jacksboro had won one more state championship in football in the time since I left, and that was in 1971. But by the late '70s, the school's football program had hit the skids. The team suffered through a 0-10 season in 1978, which is what it had done the year before I first started coaching there, way back in the late '50s. In my first year back, we went 4-6, so we won four more

Chuck gives instructions to his Cleburne players during a timeout in the team's win over Brownwood at Amon G. Carter Stadium, October 16, 1982. *Photo by John Costello, courtesy* Fort Worth Star-Telegram *Photograph Collection, Special Collections, University of Texas at Arlington Library, Arlington, Texas.*

games than the previous year. We ended up as district champs in 1980, the second year I was there. We went 7-2-2, and we got the ball rollin' again.

Meanwhile, my principal at Jacksboro, Don Smith, took the superintendent's job in the Cleburne school district in 1981. He called me and said, "We haven't had a winning season in 10 years here at Cleburne. There's two things I want done before I die. I want us to have a winning season, and I want us to beat Coach Gordon Wood at Brownwood. We'll pay you well for it."

That was a tough spot for me to be in, because Jacksboro had been loyal to me and helped me get going. I weighed the situation, and I saw there was no way I could win. It wasn't time for me to leave Jacksboro just after we got them going again. But on the other hand, Don was a great superintendent and school person, and we were best friends when he was principal at Jacksboro, so I couldn't turn him down.

In the end, I decided to leave Jacksboro and go to Cleburne, and naturally the Jacksboro folks were mad at me for leaving again. I left them once for Garland, and now I was leaving them again for Cleburne. I didn't blame them for being mad. It took a few years to get some of my Jacksboro friends back after I left.

On top of that, my quarterback on the 1980 district champion Jacksboro team, Dean Sullivan, moved to Cleburne the same year I started coaching there in 1981. It just so happened that his mom and dad had divorced around that time, and his daddy lived in Cleburne. It was a coincidence. I didn't recruit him to go to Cleburne, like I'm sure some people thought. Dean moved down there to be with his daddy. Later, his mother and her husband moved to Cleburne, too.

Dean was not only a great quarterback, but he was also a great hurdler. I had all my quarterbacks run the hurdles, since that's what I ran in high school. It really helped with stretchin' them out and gettin' them in shape. All my quarterbacks were outstanding hurdlers. In fact, one year when I was at Cleburne, my quarterbacks finished 1-2-3 in hurdles at the district track meet.

I've always worn a cowboy hat. People think I'm naked without it. I stood out on the sidelines when I was coaching football because I'm 6-foot-5 and I had that cowboy hat on. One of the things I did to fire the crowd up during football games was take my cowboy hat off and wave it while I was standing on the sideline. It played a big part in getting the fans involved.

A lot of people think the hat wave started when I coached at Garland, but it didn't start until my first year at Cleburne in 1981.

We didn't have to do anything like that in Garland to get people fired up—it was usually a sellout, and they were great, great crowds. All we had to do was get the Garland people to the game, and they did the firing up all by themselves. But at Cleburne we had to wake them up.

When I took the job at Cleburne, I felt like it was better to get the junior high kids and faculty on our side first, so that's where I went. One day they had a pep rally at the junior high, so I went over there and spoke. I told the crowd of kids, "We have a secret we're going to do Friday night at the ballgame, and y'all are going to be it. We want every one of you to be there and we want you to bring your mom and dad, too. We're going to do something special, and it's going to be you doing it. Whenever I raise my hat, I want y'all to holler the loudest you can and make sure that whoever brought you there is hollering, too. Y'all are the only ones who know about this. Don't tell any of those high school students up there." Of course, the first thing they did was tell the high school kids.

When Friday night came, they were all primed and ready. Just before the opening kickoff, I stepped up there and raised that hat, and they let it out. The junior high kids, the high school kids, the moms and dads, and even some of the oldsters in town got into it. That was how one of my signature moves, the "hat wave," was born.

It was that way from then on.

It's a good thing it was that way, because we needed all the fan support we could get. We especially needed it when we played our biggest rival, Brownwood High School in Central Texas, which was coached by the legendary Gordon Wood.

By the early 1980s, Gordon had coached at Brownwood for more than twenty years and had won seven state championships there. At the time I went to Cleburne to coach in 1981, Cleburne had not beaten his Brownwood team since 1964. It's no wonder beating Gordon Wood was on Don Smith's bucket list.

Gordon and I were both winners whose football teams had won multiple state championships. He had in fact won nine, including two at Stamford High School in the '50s before he got to Brownwood. We both wore a hat, except he wore a fedora and I wore a cowboy hat.

But that was where the similarities ended. We were pretty much enemies when we were coaching against each other. I didn't want us to be, but we were.

Maybe Gordon felt like his run of district titles or his streak against Cleburne was in jeopardy now that I was coaching at Cleburne—I don't know. He was one of the "founding fathers" of Texas high school football as we know it, and he could not stand losing.

All I knew was that he tried every way in the world to get us kicked out of the league for alleged recruiting violations. He was never able to convince anyone in power that we had done

Chuck greets North Side High School head coach Danny Lamb before the game on November 13, 1982. Cleburne won over North Side 38-7. *Photo by Paul Moseley, courtesy* Fort Worth Star-Telegram *Photograph Collection, Special Collections, University of Texas at Arlington Library, Arlington, Texas.*

August 8, 1983. Chuck checks his stopwatch during one of Cleburne's first practices in preparation for the fall season. *Photo by Rob Clark Jr., courtesy* Fort Worth Star-Telegram *Photograph Collection, Special Collections, University of Texas at Arlington Library, Arlington, Texas.*

anything wrong. He knew my history with Jacksboro and with Garland, and that prompted him to call me a "hired gun" when I came to Cleburne. It didn't take long for our rivalry to spread statewide—and when your rivalry covers a state as big as Texas, that is one big rivalry.

Cleburne and Brownwood played in District 4-4A at that time. Brownwood usually tore that district up and almost always won it. My first year at Cleburne, we played Brownwood away. We had them on the ropes, but it got away from us. With Dean Sullivan as quarterback, we went 7-3, so we had a winning season at Cleburne.

The second year, I was looking for a way to get our kids motivated to beat Brownwood, and that's when we started "The Countdown."

(Above left) Chuck gives instructions during Cleburne's playoff win over Lubbock Estacado High School, Wichita Falls, December 5, 1982. (Above right) Coach Curtis and his Cleburne players leave the field following their playoff victory over Lubbock Estacado. Cleburne won the game 7-0. *Photos by Larry C. Price, courtesy* Fort Worth Star-Telegram *Photograph Collection, Special Collections, University of Texas at Arlington Library, Arlington, Texas.*

By 1982, we'd got the football program rollin' at Cleburne and got a bunch of the kids to try out that hadn't been out for football before. Some were basketball players, or just were not in sports at all when they came out for football.

That got us started. I thought, maybe we should do something goofy. As a football coach, the goal is to focus on one game at a time and never look any further ahead than the next game. That's what you preach to your team, also. But all that went out the window with Brownwood on the schedule for the seventh game of the season. We had the date of the Brownwood game, October 16, circled on our calendar from the first day of workouts. We started the countdown sixty to seventy days before we played them. Every day, the newspaper and the local radio station would count down one more day. "Folks, it's only fifty more days 'til we beat Brownwood." Then it got down to forty, then it got down to a month, then a week. Then it got down to a few days. This was crazy. It really was.

Chuck discusses the game plan on the sidelines during Cleburne's
game with Brownwood at Amon G. Carter Stadium, October 16, 1982.
Photo by John Costello, courtesy Fort Worth Star-Telegram *Photograph
Collection, Special Collections, University of Texas at Arlington Library,
Arlington, Texas.*

The countdown caused some major excitement in the town
of Cleburne. When it got to within a few days of the October 16
game date, I realized there was no way we could handle all the
people that were stirred up. Gordon Wood could already see it
coming. He thought that in the process of firing everyone up that
we had broken some rules, and that got Gordon and me spatting
at each other. We hadn't broken any rules, but he was looking for
any advantage he could get because he knew this was going to be
one tough game for his Brownwood team. Both teams were 5-1
headed into the game, so both of us knew the winner of this game
would be in the driver's seat for the district title.

Gordon made the two-hour trip up to Cleburne from Brownwood and told us he wanted half of the seats in our stadium.
Like a lot of high school football stadiums, the visitors' side at
Cleburne was really small and our side, the home side, was really
big. So in order for Brownwood to have half the seats, some of
their fans would have to sit on the home side.

I told Gordon, "You can have half the seats on our side if

you want. But we're sold out on our side and you'll have to go to those people and get the tickets from them."

Well, he couldn't very well start asking our fans to give up their tickets. In fact, I started to think that our stadium might not even hold all the Cleburne fans for this one, since everyone in town was so fired up. So I came up with a solution that would accommodate everyone who wanted to see the game.

I thought we might as well move this game to Amon G. Carter Stadium at TCU, if they would allow it. Fortunately for us, TCU was playing on the road that Saturday. TCU said okay, so we just moved the game to Fort Worth. The crowd there was estimated at over twenty-five thousand. Some high-profile state champion-ship games and even playoff games can draw that many, but a crowd that size was unheard of for a regular-season 4A football game in Texas. If anyone doubted the magnitude of the rivalry between Gordon and me, a crowd of more than twenty-five thou-sand for a regular season game should have provided conclusive evidence.

Robby White received the opening kickoff for us and ran it back forty yards to midfield. This set up a thirty-six-yard field goal by Kyle Sims on our first drive of the game. We led 3-0 heading into halftime. Brownwood received the second half kick-off, but our linebacker, Ken Cunningham, recovered a fumble in Brownwood territory. Peter Pope eventually punched it into the end zone from a yard out, but we missed the extra point. We were up, 9-0, just minutes into the second half.

We dominated time of possession in the first three quarters and kept the Brownwood offense off the field for the most part. In the fourth quarter, they tried to get back in it, though. They kicked a field goal with about nine minutes left to cut our lead to 9-3.

I put more pressure on our kids, especially our defense, and they responded well. Late in the fourth quarter, Brownwood fielded a punt on about the one-yard line. They had ninety-nine yards to go, but they made ten on a running play to give them some breathing room. To prevent them from breaking out with a big gain, we made sure we had our best tacklers in the second-

October 16, 1982: Coach Curtis raises his famous cowboy hat in celebration with Cleburne High School players and fans after Cleburne's win over Gordon Wood's Brownwood team. *Photo by John Costello, courtesy* Fort Worth Star-Telegram *Photograph Collection, Special Collections, University of Texas at Arlington Library, Arlington, Texas.*

ary while the linemen up front put the pressure on. We played an extra linebacker so that if Brownwood used a running play, we'd have a better chance of stopping it.

They marched the ball right down the field and took it deep into Cleburne territory, but our defense came through for us again. Our quarterback Rodney Fowler, who also played safety for us, hit their receiver and forced a fumble inside the ten-yard line. Cunningham was there to fall on it on the four-yard line, for his second fumble recovery of the game. That gave us the ball with about a minute remaining. After that, we just had to take two kneel-downs, and the game was over.

We won the game, 9-3. Gordon and I didn't say much to each other when we met at midfield after the game. Just before he came out to midfield, he was getting oxygen on the sideline.

That game ranks up there with the state championships my Jacksboro and Garland teams won. Winning that game was like winning two state championships in a row. I was fortunate that

Coach Curtis with a couple of his former players circa 2004: Gene Mayes, left, played for Chuck on both state championship teams at Garland in the '60s and also played at TCU, then was an assistant coach under Chuck at Cleburne; and Gene's son, Allen, at right, played for Chuck at Cleburne and played at TCU. In front is Allen's son, Alex, who as of 2014 is on the University of Minnesota football team as a sophomore.

we won that game against Brownwood, because it preserved the countdown. I would have looked bad if they had blown us out.

Just as we expected, that win decided the district champion for 4A. Cleburne won it with a 9-1 record, and Brownwood finished second. Cleburne went all the way to the state semifinal before we lost to Corsicana, 7-3. The following year, in 1983, we beat Brownwood again, this time on the road, by the score of 28-13, so I beat Gordon two out of the three times I played him. That had never been done before. He accused us of this and that, but we beat him fair and square both times. Gordon brought out the best in our kids at Cleburne, because we all wanted to beat him.

Gordon Wood was seventy-one years old when he retired after the 1985 season with three hundred and ninety-six career wins, at that time more than any other high school football coach in Texas. In forty-five years as a head coach, he lost only ninety-one games and tied fifteen, which gave him a winning percentage

Chuck rallies his troops during University of Texas at
Arlington's football practice in August 1984. *Photo by
Stuart Wong, courtesy* Fort Worth Star-Telegram *Photograph
Collection, Special Collections, University of Texas at
Arlington Library, Arlington, Texas.*

of better than eighty percent. He died in 2003 at age eighty-nine.
His autobiography was called *Coach of the Century*. And he was.

After three years of coaching at Cleburne, in 1984, I was offered the head coaching job at the University of Texas at Arlington, about halfway between Dallas and Fort Worth. Obtaining a
head coaching position at a university had been a goal of mine
for many, many years. I almost got my wish when I was an assistant coach at SMU in 1966. At that time, the University of
Oklahoma was making a coaching change. They had a couple of
disappointing years since their legendary coach, Bud Wilkinson,
had retired, and they had just let the new coach go. When the
OU job opened up, I interviewed and thought I did a good job of
selling myself. I made the final three, and I felt like I was going to
get the job.

There was just one problem. The owner of the oil rig where I
worked when I was in high school at Gainesville was still on the
board of regents for OU. The guy who tried to talk me into going
to OU instead of TCU, more than ten years earlier. I heard from
a couple of OU guys I'd gotten acquainted with that this guy was
going to pull his financial support from OU if they hired me.

Chuck surveys his team on the practice field during the week leading up to his first game as UTA coach in September 1984. *Photo by Stuart Wong, courtesy* Fort Worth Star-Telegram *Photograph Collection, Special Collections, University of Texas at Arlington Library, Arlington, Texas.*

I didn't get the job.

Instead they hired Jim Mackenzie, who was an assistant coach from Arkansas. But after only one year at OU, Mackenzie died of a heart attack in 1967 at age thirty-seven. So I thought, "You know, I'm glad I didn't get that job."

It took me another eighteen years after missing out on the OU job, but I finally I landed my first college head coaching job. The people at UTA knew about the Cleburne-Brownwood rivalry and how we drew crowds to our games by stirring the pot, and they needed that at UTA to get the students and locals fired up about

September 9, 1984: Coach Curtis instructs his UTA team on the sidelines during his first game as UTA head coach. UTA defeated West Texas A&M 27-19, and went on to post a 7-4 record for the season. *Photo by Jerry Hoefer, courtesy* Fort Worth Star-Telegram *Photograph Collection, Special Collections, University of Texas at Arlington Library, Arlington, Texas.*

our football team. The UTA Mavericks had won the Southland Conference in 1981, but had suffered through a couple of losing seasons by the time I started there. I knew how to recruit, and I knew there was plenty of football talent in the area. My quarterback, Phil Blue, who ended up coaching for me later while I was the athletic director in Mineral Wells, was a great all-around athlete. We seemed to be primed for success.

My first year there in 1984, we won seven games and lost only four, to finish in third place in our conference. My second year, we lost the last two games of the season in the final seconds, and finished 4-6-1. If we had won those last two games, we would have finished 6-4-1 and won the conference championship.

I thought I would stay at UTA for a long time, but school administrators pulled the plug on the football program just as I was starting my third year there. The football team wasn't making money, but we were drawing better than they'd ever drawn. Unfortunately for us, the president of the university was an engineer and not an athletics man. To him it was all about dollars and cents.

Coach Curtis addresses the media after the announcement that the football program at the University of Texas at Arlington was being eliminated, November 26, 1985. Chuck spent two seasons as UTA's head coach. *Photo by Joe Giron, courtesy* Fort Worth Star-Telegram *Photograph Collection, Special Collections, University of Texas at Arlington Library, Arlington, Texas.*

I thought for sure that another college would call and offer me a job, but for some reason it never happened. It ended up being my last college coaching job. That wasn't the way I wanted my career as a college coach to end, but it was all right.

The way it ended at UTA kind of took all the fun out of coaching for me, and I had to take a break from it. I spent most of 1986 on my ranch in Millsap, Texas, tending to my horses and cattle. UTA was paying me that whole time, because when the administrators cut the football program, I still had a year left on my contract.

After a year away from coaching, I decided to get back into it. I had a choice between two schools in the Fort Worth area, Mansfield High School or Aledo High School. I should have taken Mansfield, but Aledo was small and it was pretty close to where I owned some land, so I went with Aledo.

In 1986, the year before I arrived, the Aledo Bearcats were 6-4 but they missed the playoffs. In 1987, my first year, we had

Chuck sold conversion vans in between coaching gigs.
Photo by Norm Tindell, courtesy Fort Worth Star-Telegram
*Photograph Collection, Special Collections, University of Texas
at Arlington Library, Arlington, Texas.*

a winning season and the team made the playoffs for the first time in six years, finishing at 6-5 overall. In my second season, we were 8-3 and qualified for the postseason again. Even though we lost in the first round of the playoffs both times, I had two winning seasons and two playoff appearances at Aledo in the two years I was there.

Despite the success we were having on the field, coaching at Aledo turned out to be a mistake for me. The local sportswriter owned the little newspaper he wrote for, and Aledo was a small town. He came to me one day and told me that he was against me getting the head coaching job at Aledo High School because he believed that my salary was too high and that I was costing the school district too much money. Because he felt that way, it was hard to get any positive articles in the local paper about me or the football team. It seemed like almost all the press was negative. So I eased out of there after two years. Aledo didn't make the playoffs again for another eight years after I left.

That was my last coaching job. When I left Aledo, I decided to retire from coaching at age fifty-three in 1988. My final career

Chuck puts the finishing touches on another car sale in January 1987, just a few short months before he became the head football coach at Aledo High School. *Photo by Dale Blackwell, courtesy* Fort Worth Star-Telegram *Photograph Collection, Special Collections, University of Texas at Arlington Library, Arlington, Texas.*

coaching record was 135-41-3, a winning percentage of .754, with three consecutive state championships from 1962-64. The first two of those, '62 and '63, came at different schools in different classifications—Jacksboro in 2A and Garland in 4A. Both of those state championship games were shutouts—52-0 over Rockdale for Jacksboro in '62 and 17-0 over Corpus Christi Miller for Garland in '63. Then we came from behind to beat Galena Park in 1964.

It took thirty-five years for Garland to win another state championship, this time in Class 5A, in 1999. I kept up with the Garland team that year. In fact, I was down in Houston with Homer Johnson when they won the championship game against Katy. They got to play indoors at the Astrodome. I gave the team a pep talk before the state championship game. Homer asked me if I wanted to talk to the team before the game or at halftime, so I told him I wanted to do it before the game. It was a tough one for me. I just told them what we did when I coached at Garland thirty-five years earlier. We didn't bully our opponents or brag— we just did it by playing as a team and letting our play on the

Chuck instructs his Aledo High School players during Aledo's game against Mineral Wells, September 18, 1988. Mineral Wells won this game 33-28. This was Chuck's last year to be a high school head football coach. Later he became athletic director at Mineral Wells High School. *Photo by Brian R. McLean, courtesy* Fort Worth Star-Telegram *Photograph Collection, Special Collections, University of Texas at Arlington Library, Arlington, Texas.*

field do the talking for us. We were prepared mentally and didn't make many mistakes that encouraged our opponents. When you don't make mistakes, you don't beat yourself. I just told them to stay mentally sharp and energized.

I finished my pep talk, and then I got out of the way and watched them. Garland won it, 37-25, over Katy. And they came from behind to do it, just like my Garland team did against Galena Park in '64. The '99 Garland team had trailed Katy, 19-14, at halftime.

Winning brings happiness, winning brings electricity, and winning brings you to where you don't get tired. When you're winning, you're right at the top of your game physically and mentally. Half the time, kids will question someone who's above them, like a coach. But the kids I coached never questioned me on why we did this or why we did that. I was fortunate to have the respect of the players and parents throughout my coaching career. When I gave instructions to do something, they did it. They worked harder and were successful, and that was our payday. I think they realized how much I cared about them individually and as a team. I believe they knew that I had their best interests at heart.

I'm not a disciplinarian. I always let my players know what we expected of them, but as far as declaring "Thou shalt not do this" or "Thou shalt not do that"—that wasn't me. I tried to get enough information to them so that they would want to be at their best and they would want to win a state championship. I always told the kids, "I want all your abilities and your thought channels, and you police yourself, because you're the only one who can determine right or wrong for you. That's the way we're going to win the state championship this year." As it turned out, things did work out—my teams won three state championships in a row.

With that philosophy, I never had any discipline problems in all my years of coaching. That was the same philosophy that my college coach Abe Martin used. We wanted to win for him. He made us feel special, and we wanted to do what was right not just for us but also for him.

To have a winning team, each one of your players needs to be in the same thinking category. When you've got everybody pulling in the same direction, you've got a team effort. If you're working two old mules and you're planting your garden, both of them need to be pulling an equal load and not letting one or the other carry the whole load. Each one of us was responsible for carrying his own part of the load. As we won, it was certainly easier to put the philosophy over to the kids. We knew we could accomplish more working together as a team than a single individual can accomplish.

CHAPTER FOUR

LIFE AFTER COACHING

We had an unfortunate situation in 1964 (at Garland High School) where someone tried to sue both me and Chuck. On the day of the state semifinal game against Amarillo Tascosa at the Cotton Bowl in Dallas, we were supposed to meet with the people who were suing us and their lawyer at eight in the morning. Garland was scheduled to play Tascosa at the Cotton Bowl at two o'clock that afternoon, so Chuck didn't have any time to be fiddling around with a lawsuit. He was mad about having to do that.

Before the meeting, earlier that morning, Chuck and I went up to my office in the administration building to plan our strategy. At that time my office was up in the barracks on the Garland High School campus. We planned exactly what we were going to do and exactly what we were going to say in this meeting.

When it was time for the meeting, we got up and walked around the corner, and Chuck, who was wearing his trademark ten-gallon hat, raised his hands in the air as we walked. I thought, "He's going to try to fly out of there and leave me to take care of this."

Chuck's dad was an Assembly of God preacher. As we sat down for the meeting, Chuck said, "Let's start this meeting with a word of prayer."

So he prayed, and he prayed, and prayed, and prayed about everything he knew about and part of what he didn't. I was dreading when he was going to quit, because I knew as soon as he was finished, we were going to catch heck. But he kept praying and praying, and finally he just wore out and he stopped.

When Chuck finished praying, the person who was going to sue us walked over to me and said, "Mr. Johnson, we're certainly sorry to have troubled you gentlemen. Let's forget this whole matter."

HOMER B. JOHNSON, *Athletic Director,*
Garland Independent School District

I n 1991, three years after I left coaching, I took a job as the first full-time athletic director for the Mineral Wells Independent School District, about forty-five miles west of Fort Worth. And that's when I first met Carole.

Carole has been a real blessing in my life. We are on the same team, pulling in the same direction. We've been a team for twenty years now, and counting.

She had seen me once back in 1982 at the Cleburne-Brownwood game at TCU. She was in the stands that day, and she saw me down on the sideline. When I waved my hat and the crowd went wild, she said she had to take a closer look.

We finally met about nine years later. In 1991, the first spring I was athletic director in Mineral Wells, I went to San Angelo in West Texas for the district track meet. She was a math teacher at Mineral Wells High School at that time, and her son was competing in the track meet. I met her, but that was as far as it went at the time. Her husband was assistant superintendent or something. He was in the "big house," which was what we called the administration building. Although neither one of us realized it, Carole and I were both going through divorces at around the same time.

Carole's math classroom was down the hall from my office at the high school. After some time had passed, I would go by her room and say, "I left my keys in my truck. Could you come by and open my door for me?" or "You know what, I lost my key. Could you open my door this morning?"

I think she caught on to it, so I slacked off a little bit. We did some talking, but we never got serious until I called her for a date.

The first time I called her, I didn't think she was going to answer because she thought maybe I was going to ask her to come back to coaching. She had previously coached track and girls basketball in Mineral Wells, but she didn't want to do any more coaching. By that time, she had left Mineral Wells High School and was teaching at North Richland Hills, northeast of

Chuck and Carole Curtis, circa 1994,
shortly after they were married.

Fort Worth. I waited for a brief period of time, and then I called her once again. That's when she decided, well, she hadn't had a free meal in a while, so she gave me a try. I didn't mention anything about trying to hire her again as a coach. Instead I said, "I'm needing to go to a few functions, and I need the best looking gal in town to go with me. What time do you want me to pick you up tonight?" She thought and said, "Seven or seven-thirty will be fine."

I went and picked her up in Fort Worth and we just started back over to the Northside. We went to a club and danced a few licks. She liked the way I was dancing, and I liked the way she was dancing, so it worked out pretty well. And that's how we kicked it off.

From there, we did a lot of talking on the phone, and things just started working out. We were married on December 31, 1993, at my Turkey Creek Ranch just outside of Mineral Wells.

Chuck and Carole enjoying a laugh together
at a Garland High School reunion in 2005.
Photo courtesy Steve Rhodes.

The ceremony took place on the deck overlooking the ranch. Carole said she picked that date, New Year's Eve, so I would remember it.

In 2003, after ten years of marriage, we renewed our wedding vows. I guess we were looking for an excuse to have a cookout. We renewed our vows at the Turkey Creek Ranch where we were originally married. Our preacher at the time, Pastor Mark Bumpus of the First Baptist Church of Mineral Wells, officiated the ceremony.

By the time we renewed our vows, I had retired as athletic director for the Mineral Wells Independent School District. I accomplished what I needed to there—in 2000, I was instrumental in upgrading the facilities for all sports, girls and boys. We have some great facilities there now.

In 2004, we moved into a comfortable home on ten acres just a few miles from downtown Mineral Wells. We have a barn on our property where I keep my horses, and it's a great location. From where we live, I can go anywhere and do business. We're close to the Dallas-Fort Worth Metroplex, but we live out in the country.

Mineral Wells ISD was declared a "poor" school district by the state at that time. Since we were "poor," we would get a larger amount of money from the state for our schools than richer

Chuck shown at his Turkey Creek Ranch
just outside of Mineral Wells, circa 2006.
Photo by Pete Kendall, courtesy of the
Cleburne Times-Review.

districts would. We knew the oil boom was coming, though, and it would most likely be the last time that we would be deemed a poor school district.

The state paid for sixty percent of our improvement programs. That helped pay for our football stadium, track, weight rooms, workout facility, and many other things. I'm proud of that.

The people in Mineral Wells didn't understand that the state was paying for sixty percent of it. They only knew the cost of the new facilities exceeded what we could pay on our own. So the people in Mineral Wells voted to fire my school board. It had taken me about eight to ten years to get the right people on the board that had enough courage to okay this project. All we could say then was that we got what we needed and wanted, and it wasn't costing our community but forty percent. Our taxes didn't go up.

Chuck enjoys an afternoon on his porch in Mineral Wells.

After we got those new facilities, all my goals I had set going into that job were accomplished. So it was time for me to get out of the way and let someone fresh take over. I retired from that position in 2001, after ten years on the job, and I moved into the next phase of my life.

One of the things I wanted to do after I retired as the athletic director in Mineral Wells was concentrate on my horses. I've always owned horses and I've always loved riding. Over the years I had won a lot of money in shows and cutting horse contests. I began competing in cutting horse contests around 1970 at weekend shows in Seymour, Texas, which is close to being halfway between Dallas and Lubbock. I competed in shows mostly on weekends all over Texas.

For two years in the 1980s, I served as the president of the local chapter of the West Central Texas Cutting Horse Association. Membership increased by almost fifty percent while I was president. A few years ago, I was inducted into the West Central Texas Cutting Horse Hall of Fame after Lynn Strickland nominated me for the honor. I had met Lynn years earlier when I first became involved in cutting horse contests. We became fast friends because

Chuck, shown here in 1995, was instrumental in
getting new athletic facilities for the Mineral Wells
ISD during his time as the athletic director.
Photo courtesy Steve Rhodes.

we shared a love of horses, and he already knew who I was when
we met because he had attended college at TCU a couple of years
after I graduated.

Cutting horse contests are derived from late nineteenth-cen-
tury ranching in West Texas, and they officially began having
contests in the 1940s. It is a big-money venture nowadays; people
come to Texas from all over the country to participate.

In a cutting horse contest, you have a group of cattle and you
have four helpers. There are two cattle holders and two horses
further back into the arena, into the middle. These are to keep the
cattle in a grouped area. The cutter comes down with the horse
really slow and easy and he eases into the herd and picks one cow
out. He brings the steer on out in front and then turns his horse
loose. His horse does the cutting, keeping that cow from getting
back into the herd. You can cue him a little bit if the judge doesn't
see it, but most of the time he's going to see it. That cow wants to
get back into the herd, but the horse jumps back and forth, back

Chuck is shown competing in a cutting horse contest in Fort Worth in the early 1980s.

Chuck Curtis was named to the West Central Texas Cutting Horse Hall of Fame for his success in cutting horse contests and his work with horses.

and forth, all on his own. After you've trained your horse and you can bring that cow out, you just throw the reins to the horse and let them hang down, and once you get the back end of him, he'll keep that cow from going back into the herd. The one that does it the prettiest or the best wins. There is a point system that you can build up. You'll cut about three cows, and you have to do it within about a two-and-a-half-minute period.

My favorite horse, Boss, won the most money. In fact, I rode Boss almost exclusively throughout my cutting horse career. Lynn

Chuck tips his hat while he rides his favorite horse, Boss, near the Turkey Creek Ranch circa 2006. *Photo by Pete Kendall, courtesy of the* Cleburne Times-Review.

Strickland gave Boss to me when the horse was about five years old in the late '80s, and we really hit it off. I've had a jillion horses, but Boss was always my favorite. He was always so easily trainable. Everything you asked him to do, he was willing to do it, and he wanted to do it, too. He reminded me of a perfect kid. He would play around with you when you wanted him to or he would get serious when you wanted him to. We started going to the bigger shows when I landed him and we just kept a-winnin' and a-winnin'. The money he won paid for all our feed for the other horses, and he really got us going in the cutting horse business. After Boss led a long, productive life, we finally had to put him down when he was thirty years old, in late 2013.

Not only was I able to concentrate more on horses and cutting contests after I retired, I even found a way to get a job that

Chuck and son Brad Spencer celebrated with grandkids
Cole (with trophy) and Vaughn in 2008, after Cole's team
won the Pee Wee Super Bowl in Gibsonia, Pennsylvania.

involved horses. When Carole and I settled into our house in
Mineral Wells in 2004, I still wasn't ready to retire, even though
I was sixty-nine years old. So I went to work as a salesman for a
family-owned feed business, Gorman Milling, in Gorman, about
sixty miles southwest of Fort Worth.

I didn't know anybody in Gorman. Gorman Milling ran an
ad in the paper in Mineral Wells, so I just cut out the ad and
decided I'd drive down there. I called first to see if the person
who was hiring was there. We called the head of the family, the
"daddy rabbit," and he was there working every day, though his
sons were in their forties and fifties. He said, "It's like a vacation.
I've always enjoyed this."

The daddy rabbit had all of his sons fixed right according to
their abilities and their personalities The one that I worked under
had a salesman's personality. The other two had more back-in-
the-mill type, overseeing-things personalities.

My sales territory was North Central Texas. Most of the feed
we sold was for horses and cattle, but we had almost every kind
of animal feed. We also sold feed for goats, lambs, deer, hogs,

TCU Chancellor Victor Boschini with
Chuck in 2007—the 50-year reunion of
the Class of 1957.

dogs, and cats. We even sold chicken scratch. We also sold acces-
sories like feeding troughs, overhead bins, and tubs.

A lot of my customers were horse cutters in the Weatherford
area. Weatherford is the cutting horse capital of the world. That's
the town's saying and it's true, because all the major cuttings take
place in or near Fort Worth. I knew a lot of those cutters, since I
cut. They knew me and trusted me, and that helped the business
out a lot. If they'd sent someone from New York down here to do
my job, they'd have run him off.

I had feed trucks coming to Weatherford and the surround-
ing areas every day. There were two to four trucks carrying and
anywhere from semi loads to pickup loads. The customers didn't
have to touch the feed, they could just shoot it into the self-feed-
ers. The cattle owners wanted the cattle to gain weight, so they
let them eat all they wanted to.

I spent a lot of time with my customers. I spoiled them, or I
tried to, anyway. Some of them had some old feeders and were
losing a lot of the feed on the ground. When you put the feed in
the feeders, you want all of it going to the cattle. I got in with the
manufacturing company that made feeders just the other side of
Jacksboro. We had already been buying those types of feeders,

98

Former University of Oklahoma and Dallas Cowboys head coach Barry Switzer offers Chuck Curtis congratulations on being named to the Texas High School Football Hall of Fame in 2007.

and with those I could help our people get a feeder in there that would be much better than their homemade ones.

I tried to make my sales routes where I could see as many customers as I could, three to four days a week. I would double check to make sure they got their orders correctly. I had to watch the weather on some of those places. We didn't want the trucks getting stuck if there was snow. We'd get a lighter truck in the case of inclement weather.

I really took care of my customers, and that's one of the reasons the company really took care of me. The customers didn't gripe and complain about not getting their feed. The only thing I really had to work to smooth over was the jump in prices for the feed. I tried to let them know as soon as I got the information from the mill that the price of the feed was going up, which most of them really understood, and they appreciated being told beforehand instead of finding out when they got the bill.

I've stayed close with Gorman Milling since I've retired. I still use their feed for my horses. When I was inducted into the Texas High School Football Hall of Fame in May 2007, my coworkers from the feed company made the two-hour trip over to Waco for the ceremony. When we counted everybody, including wives, we had about one hundred and ten people, so we filled our section up.

During the time I worked for the feed company in 2008, Carole and I started looking into the Palo Pinto County Cowboy Church in Mineral Wells. We had worshipped at the First Baptist Church in Mineral Wells for the previous fourteen years, but we decided to look for another church when our longtime pastor, Mark Bumpus, moved on to a bigger church out in West Texas.

The Palo Pinto County Cowboy Church was just starting at that time. We discovered they needed a bass player, so I went and played with them one Sunday. I found out the people in the band could really play their instruments well. When I played with the band at the Cowboy Church, everything just clicked, because everybody could play. I don't know if it's selfish or what, but I have more fun playing with great players and blending in than I do playing with mediocre players. If you've got the teamwork going for you, it's fun. And when you play with people who are really good at what they do, it elevates your game. It's like playing football or basketball. It's more fun when you have great teammates and you're winning.

I play alongside some top-notch musicians at the Palo Pinto County Cowboy Church every Sunday. Two of those musicians, Frank Johnson on piano and Jerry Van Kirk on fiddle, were inducted into the Cowtown Society of Western Music Hall of Fame in 2010, along with me. Our steel guitar player, Albert Talley, used to play with Bob Wills and His Texas Playboys, and he is the president of the Texas Steel Guitar Association. Albert comes all the way from Cleburne to Mineral Wells, about an hour and fifteen minute drive, every Sunday to play with us. Our pastor, Roger Keck, is also our drummer in the band, and he's a heck of a drummer.

We play all kinds of music at the Palo Pinto County Cowboy Church. We play western swing, gospel, and several other types. We typically start around 10:30 every Sunday morning and play for a couple of hours. Then our pastor, Roger, moves out from behind the drum set to preach a sermon.

At the Palo Pinto County Cowboy Church, you can be yourself. Nobody worries about the jeans that you wear, or if you

Roger Keck, shown behind the pulpit in 2012, is the Cowboy Church's pastor and the drummer for the band.

wear overalls, boots, or an old cowboy hat. You're just as good as those with a new hat and a fancy pair of boots. We don't pass a collection plate, but we do give people an opportunity to participate and donate. When we baptize people, we do it in a horse trough right in front of the pulpit, so that's unique. We've got two big milk cans at the door where people can drop their tithing money or donations. When we have prayer, we don't ask folks to come up to the front. They can pray right from their seats or they can stand where they are if they wish.

To me, the Palo Pinto County Cowboy Church is exciting. It's like game day every Sunday when I go to church. I'm excited about the church, excited about the situation, and excited about hearing our pastor, Roger Keck, preach his sermons. He is a powerful speaker, and he also has a great sense of humor.

Carole was sold on the Cowboy Church from day one. Back in 2008, we felt like something great was going to happen with the church, which it did, and it is still happening. We were fortunate to have the opportunity to be a part of it. In 2008, when we started attending, we had only eight members, and now we have more than three hundred. We built the church every year mostly through word of mouth. I would stop in the post office and someone would say to me, "I hear y'all's church is sure doing good."

"Yes sir, we're growing. You need to come by and check us out."

"I plan on it."

We are the second largest church in Palo Pinto County, behind only the First Baptist Church in Mineral Wells, which has been around for more than one hundred years. They had a ninety-six-year head start on us.

The original location of the Cowboy Church was on North Highway 281, close to Interstate 20, just outside of Mineral Wells. The building we leased was a small barn that was previously used for selling cattle. Sellers would run their cattle through, and the buyers would bid on them. In the area where they sold the cattle, we put a floor down in the dirt in a pipe-fenced area, and that's where the band played.

We were able to buy another piece of property, seven acres, on 281. But it wasn't big enough for what we were doing, so we traded it to an oil company. We turned around and bought twenty-four acres, less the seven acres that we traded in, and that's where we built our main church. It's located in Santo, about fifteen minutes from where we live in Mineral Wells. At first it didn't seem like a good location to build a church because hardly any people live around that area. Our preacher, Roger, prayed to know if this was the right location. He got his answer, and Santo was the place where we built our church.

On the original twenty-four acres we bought was a double-wide manufactured home, and that double wide was away from the barn that was on the property. The barn didn't have any north or south sides closed in, so we started closing it in. We didn't have heat for the first part of the winter, so we got some propane heaters. Then the people started coming. About forty to sixty is all that barn would hold. When that got full, we got the big building started, where we are now. We can sit close to five hundred in our new space. We pretty much have the same folks each Sunday that have a habit of coming, but we put some chairs upstairs for visitors to see the service, and we've had to use that a time or two.

Just like he does every Sunday, Chuck warms up
to play bass in the Cowboy Church band.

It's been a real pleasurable deal.

It was lots of work, and it was a gamble. There were four or
five of us who guaranteed the money for the building itself when
we went to the bank. It's going so well now that I no longer need
to be a guarantor like I was. Now we have equity, and we're
ahead on our payments.

We have some really talented people in the church, and we're
making use of their talents. We're teaching kids how to ride horses,
rope, and do all the things cowboys do. But we also spend time
teaching them how to pray and how to feed themselves spiritually. We've got something there for everybody at the church, and
it keeps us busy. There are activities going on all through the
week at the Cowboy Church.

The membership of the Palo Pinto Cowboy Church grew from eight members to a few hundred within four years. Here the crowd waits for a Sunday sermon in 2012. Chuck and Carole are sitting just right of center.

We have a competitive roping team that competes in youth rodeos. We also have youth horse cuttings. Most of those kids are from ranch families, and they know a little bit about it. We've got some winners down there that are into roping big time, and we've got them working with the kids. They teach the kids the basic fundamentals. Roping is probably our biggest thing. For the ladies we have barrel racing, and they get to rope, too.

We went from eight to three hundred members in the first four years and got people in there that can do certain things, like teachers, musicians, lay ministers, and those who took leadership jobs with the rodeo team. We go to parades also. We try to get everybody from the church involved.

In addition to playing upright bass in the Cowboy Church band, I serve as an elder in the church along with Jimmy Clark and Tommy Self. We're like superintendents. We support our pastor, Roger. If there are any problems, we're there to work it out for him. It's like a football team with a blocking back. When a running back gets a good block, he runs right through the hole. The elders are like the blocking backs. We try to keep trouble away and make sure the people are enjoying their experience in the

Chuck and Carole bundled up for a trip to New York in 2004. The old Yankee Stadium, where the Giants played their home games when Chuck played for them in 1957, is in the background.

church. We fix anything that goes wrong.

Carole is unofficially over the audit team at the Cowboy Church. The audit team double checks the money coming in and makes sure it's going to the right place. The money goes to various things like the building fund, rodeo team, and other expenses. People have the choice of where to donate their money. Carole did most all of the bookkeeping by herself for a while, but we got her some help now. Our retired superintendent of schools in Mineral Wells, Ronny Collins, is also one of the auditors. He's good with figures. Carole feeds on being busy, and that's the way she is with the Cowboy Church. She's excited about it. She's got a lot of teachers coming down and going to church with us just because of her enthusiasm.

If the church membership continues to grow at this rate, some decisions will have to be made. In the past, when other cowboy churches have reached five hundred in membership, they've split and formed a new church with some of the chosen talented members. Right now, we have plenty of musicians, and we could let two or three go to another church if we were to split. I'd like to keep it going, and if we can split off a hundred and let them turn it into another five hundred, then we've got room for at least another hundred. It could work several different ways.

The members of the Palo Pinto County Cowboy Church are one big family, and that's what feels so good about it. That's what makes it such an attractive place to attend church. There is such a loving spirit there, and that's how we've been able to grow it so fast—mostly by word of mouth. Just like my football teams at Garland and Jacksboro, everyone at the Cowboy Church is on the same team, and we're all pulling together. With that team effort, the church has grown to where it is and continues to thrive.

It was through music that I became involved with the Palo Pinto County Cowboy Church. Music has always been a big part of my life, and it continues to be to this day.

When I was in college in the mid-1950s, several of us formed a band, and we called ourselves Abe's Aces, just like our outlaw softball team. In the band, I played the upright bass and we played the type of western swing music made popular by Bob Wills and His Texas Playboys in the 1930s and 1940s.

I listened to Bob Wills a lot when I was growing up, so he was a big influence on me musically. He played a fiddle and had a big band sound, and that's what I liked. Abe's Aces played at a lot of fraternity parties and banquet-type stuff. We played western swing music and we did really well, even though Elvis Presley was becoming popular around that time, 1956 or so. Elvis was known for rock and roll, but he could sing gospel music so well, and he even had my mom and dad liking him. Elvis didn't quite jump out at me like he did to my sister. It seemed like all the girls liked Elvis. All the guys were either in awe or jealous.

Recently, I formed a band in Mineral Wells called Chuck Curtis and his All-Star Band. To recruit members for my band, I did some advertising. Even though I was the "rookie" of the bunch, I went after great musicians to be members of my band. Most of them were already members of the Cowtown Society of Western Music Hall of Fame. In 2010, I was inducted into that same hall of fame and received the President's Choice Award, which helped us get the publicity we needed.

Chuck Curtis began playing western swing with various bands in the mid-1950s, while he was still a student at TCU. From left, O'Day Williams, Joe Hickey, Poss Elenburg, Chuck, and Dick Lindsey.

Our band consisted of Leon Rausch (Fort Worth, Texas) and Durwood Strube (Proctor, Texas) on vocals; Tommy Allsup (Azle, Texas) on lead guitar; Bob Boatright (Mansfield, Texas), Bob Bone (Weatherford, Texas), and Brady Bowen (Jacksboro, Texas) on the fiddle; Wayne Glasson (Rockwall, Texas) on keyboards; Larry Reed (Weatherford, Texas) on saxophone; Buddie Hrabal (Fort Worth, Texas) on steel guitar; Chris York (Fort Worth, Texas) on drums; and myself (from Mineral Wells, Texas) on the upright bass. Bone and Boatright, unfortunately, are deceased now.

We were playing some gigs and word was getting around, and we were doing pretty well. The local newspaper always did a fine job of covering us and helping us get the crowd out. Durwood also plays in a band called the Best Texas Band, and he has a following in Proctor, about seventy miles south of Mineral Wells. Sometimes they come all the way up here to watch us. We've played at barns, country clubs, some benefit shows, and lots of other places. In 2011, we played two shows a day every day for two weeks at a racetrack in New Mexico because they wanted us to play both before and after the races.

Tribute to Bob Wills & The Texas Playboys
A Ride With Bob

**BAND WILL BE MADE UP OF
WESTERN SWING HALL OF FAME**

Left to Right: Teddy Driskil, Bob Bone, Jim King, Chuck Curtis,
Charley O'Bannon, and Derwood Strube • Not pictured Albert Talley

Friday
July 28th @ 8:30pm
Holiday Hills Country Club
Buffet & Cash Bar
PUBLIC WELCOME

A flyer advertising a gig for Chuck Curtis and his
All-Star Band in 2010.

I've never charged for my band or asked for money. I play for
nothing, and I'm tickled to death to do it. When we get money
for playing, I let the rest of the band members get their cut and
that provides a little extra for them.

Our two most famous members are Leon Rausch and Tommy
Allsup. Leon is known as "The Voice of Bob Wills and the Texas
Playboys." Tommy played with both Bob Wills and Buddy Holly.
Tommy is a great lead guitar player. He can really play. Tommy
has become famous in music lore for losing a coin toss with Rich-
ie Valens for a seat on the airplane that crashed and killed Buddy
Holly, the Big Bopper, and Valens in 1959. Tommy told us that
story, and after that we called him "The Winner" because even
though he lost the coin toss, he was the lucky one who didn't
have to ride in that airplane. Holly, the Big Bopper, and Valens
were coming on so strong, drawing the crowds before that plane
crash. Buddy Holly is as popular as ever overseas, and Tommy

Chuck (on bass) and his All-Star Band, paying tribute to Bob Wills and western swing music.

still makes a trip over there to play now and then. He lets us know when he's going to be gone for two or three weeks.

For a few years, we had an annual tribute to Buddy Holly and Bob Wills in Mineral Wells at the Holiday Hills Country Club. We'd always have it the weekend before the big blowout in Turkey, Texas, which was where Bob Wills was from. Turkey is about a four-hour drive from Mineral Wells. Every April they have a big gathering where the surviving members of the Texas Playboys come back and play. People come to Turkey from all over in travel trailers or RVs and stay all week. We decided we'd do our tribute in Mineral Wells the week before they had theirs in Turkey. That way, we really caught a bunch of them on the way to Turkey and we were able to draw a crowd at the country club. People who were traveling could stop off for the weekend in Mineral Wells before things cranked up in Turkey, and they'd get to hear us play some of that Bob Wills Texas Playboys music. Leon Rausch would be there to sing with us and Tommy Allsup would play guitar with us.

Both Leon and Tommy were with us the day we played at our fiftieth class reunion at TCU in 2007. It was a big deal for us, because TCU hired us and because it was my fiftieth class reunion. We had three fiddles, two lead guitars, a saxophone, steel guitar, and my upright bass that day. It was hot and we were playing on top of a big flatbed trailer. It was on the east side of the football stadium, and the sun was comin' in and hittin' us direct. Tommy got up there to make his run with his guitar, and he just passed out. He fell right on his guitar, on his nose, and we had to stop playing so we could stop him from bleeding. I was next to the microphone, and I started calling for an ambulance. I thought he was seriously hurt.

The paramedics were only a half a block away from us, and boom, they were there and they handled him. They got Tommy in the ambulance and took him down to the emergency room. It was a scary deal, but Tommy was okay. He was getting along so well that he caught a ride back to TCU, and we played at the dance that night in the big auditorium. Of course, it was cool in there.

Since then, Tommy has moved to Tulsa, and he plays a lot up there. But whenever he's in the area, we grab him for a gig.

My college football coach, Abe Martin, once gave me some advice that applies not only to sports but to all areas of life. He always said to surround yourself with good folks and good things will happen. In football, if you're surrounded by good players, you're going to have success. It's the same thing with a band. Attitude means so much. You've got to be a team player. Not everybody can sing at once, and not everybody can be the star the same night. Some bands run into that, but we don't have any problems at all. Everyone gets an equal share of the spotlight. I am in awe of what great musicians they are. All they need to know is the key and they figure a way to play it.

I applied Abe Martin's advice to my music and I surrounded myself with good folks. And good things have happened to Chuck Curtis and his All-Star Band.

Besides music, one thing I really enjoy these days is motivational speaking. Most of my speaking engagements are at foot-

Chuck doing what he does best—firing people up and motivating them to be better. Here, he is speaking to a group of his former Garland High School football players in 2010. *Photo courtesy Steve Rhodes.*

ball banquets where the team is being honored for their accomplishments. I also do some college-type motivational speaking.

I've spoken at some business meetings that didn't have anything to do with sports, like the Truck Vista companies that bring their employees together and utilize that same game plan in the business world that I used in the sports world. Fuzzy's Taco Shop restaurants, the chain that serves fish tacos, are coming into our area and they've been quite successful. The president of the company, Alan Bush, played for me at Jacksboro in the early 1960s and his son, Chuck, played for me at Aledo. They called me to speak at their annual meeting at a resort in Oklahoma. I've been invited back each year to speak at their big meeting. I change my speech a little bit each time, but it's all meaningful in the same way.

What sets the tone of my speeches are the coaches that I had the pleasure to play under. Each person or coach can do it in different ways. When I coached, I chose to borrow a little bit from Tom Landry, from Vince Lombardi, from Bud Grant, and from Paul Brown. I borrowed a bunch from Abe Martin, my college coach. Those people were successful, and I watched every move they made and listened to everything they said. I've incorporated things from all my coaches into my motivational speeches at various times.

Chuck's uncle Marvin Curtis, at left, was a decorated veteran who was once a bodyguard for General Douglas MacArthur in World War II.

Whether it's kids or business, it makes me feel good when we help people or when they anticipate us helping them. I tell them to give it one hundred and ten percent, which is something I learned at SMU under Hayden Fry. I love to see grown people listening and getting excited.

I usually use some type of football story in my speeches. I think people can relate to sports analogies better than anything else. I use things that I used in pregame or at halftime from when I coached. I've used those things in motivational speaking and they work really well.

For example, if I'm talking to a group of sales people, I tell them the same thing I always told my football players—that we're here to win, and with all of us working together, we can do it. I try to get them to feel good about themselves. In football, if you're on offense, you have to be able to move the ball and not make mistakes and you have to do it with enthusiasm. If you do that, you're going to play your very best, and that's how you're going to get it done. It's the same with sales or any other type of work you do—if you're working with enthusiasm and "moving the ball," so to speak, making progress, and not making mis-

Chuck, in the center, and others observe while Carole teaches Sunday School to a group of kids at the Palo Pinto County Cowboy Church in 2012.

takes, then it's going to be a job well done.

You've got to take the good with the bad and the bad with the good. I'd say this, I've been on both sides of the ladder, and I'm happiest when I'm doing the work I'm doing now, like I'm doing in church, and helping others who need help. I'm not looking to better myself in any form or fashion, I'm helping someone else who is down to get up. I still enjoy motivational-type speaking and letting those people hear my testimony, especially the young people. I look forward to some of that during football season when the football banquets start coming around.

I always used to tell my football players, "Regardless of your past, your future is a clean slate." The longer I live, the more I realize the impact of attitude on life. Attitude to me is more important than facts. It is more important to me than the past, than education, than money, than circumstances, than failures, than successes, than what other people think or say or do. It is more important than appearance, giftedness, or skill. Attitude will make or break a company, a church, or home.

The remarkable thing is that we have a choice every day regarding the attitude we will embrace for the day. We cannot change our past. We cannot change the fact that people will act in a certain way. We cannot change the inevitable. The only thing we can do is control our own attitude. I am convinced that life is 10 percent what happens to me and 90 percent how I react to it. And so it is with all of us: we are in charge of our attitudes.

I'd like to be remembered for the good I've done and not for the bad. I'm not that man I used to be. I'm a completely different man now. In reality, I'm different, and it's for the best. Before I was putting myself first; it was all about me. Now, it's all about God and how I can serve Him.

As I've said before, football is more fun when you're winning. Anything is more fun when you're winning, and that includes life.

I was blessed to be in the right place at the right time several times in my football coaching career, and even after my coaching career was over, too.

I've played for and coached winning football teams, but there is another winning team that is more important that any other team in football or any sport, and that is Jesus Christ's team.

I'm playing for the winning team now and my wife, Carole, is right there with me. I believe that God preserved me to this age so that I could do what I'm doing now in helping to spread the good news. We've helped get a lot of people into church. We've really worked at it, and we've got our priorities in order. You could definitely say I've gone from the spread formation to spreading the word.

THANKS AND PRAISES

Chuck's family gathered to celebrate Chuck's election to the Texas High School Football Hall of Fame in 2007. Pictured here are Joann and Brad Spencer (daughter-in-law and son), wife Carole, Caleb Amis (grandson), Terry Amis (son-in-law), Kim Amis (daughter), Lara Amis (granddaughter), and Chuck.

I have been truly blessed.

The good Lord has seen fit to bless me—my life—in so many ways. Of all the gifts He has blessed me with, the one I am perhaps the most thankful for is the gift of free will. It is because of this gift that I have been blessed to experience all that life has to offer—both the good and the bad. I would not be the man I am today without God, and I thank Him every day for the blessings and lessons He has seen fit to share with me.

The Lord has blessed my life with so many incredible people, who always arrived when they were needed most. They are almost too numerous to name; yet while I hate to leave anyone out, there are those who must be mentioned and thanked for their presence in my life.

W.A. Thomas, of Holliday, Texas, for taking a chance on a rookie coach.

Don Smith, past superintendent of Cleburne ISD, for support and positive influences.

Homer Johnson, Garland ISD athletic director, and my "Gang from Garland." The support and encouragement from my AD and players have never waned, even as the years have passed.

Dr. Ronny Collins, retired superintendent of Mineral Wells ISD, and his wife, Terri. It wouldn't be much of a stretch to say this book might not exist if had not been for their support (and photographic skills).

All my assistant coaches over the years. You have blessed the lives of all you worked with through your dedication to both the kids and the sport.

My family at the Palo Pinto County Cowboy Church. Bless you all for being my family.

My lovely daughter, Kim, who I have finally forgiven for graduating from UT.

Our Pittsburgh kids, especially my stepson, Brad. Actually, just forget about the "step" part. I love you, son.

My wife Carole's family has been incredibly loving and supporting.

Behind every great man, they say, is a great woman. I am blessed to have my great woman beside me. Carole, you are my everything. Thank you for being my partner and my best friend.

—Chuck Curtis